Jim Carroll's latest book is a lifeline for those of us being whipsawed by the wired world. It's a relentless and often intimidating experience. Jim's tone is empathetic, his explanations inspire even those of us who are the last of the Luddites.

Pamela Wallin,
CBC's *Pamela Wallin Live*

Jim Carroll has done it again! This new book encourages, inspires and offers confidence to all of us who grew up playing hockey on a pond, instead of computer games."

Frank McKenna,
Premier of New Brunswick

"*If you're wondering why you seem to be having trouble getting excited about the digital revolution, Jim Carroll has a book for you. Packed with insights, stories and vignettes (some quite hilarious) you will learn that you're not alone and that there is still hope for our generation and for you to muddle into the digital world."*

Don Tapscott, Chairman of the Alliance for Converging Technologies. Best-selling author, including *The Digital Economy* and the upcoming *Growing Up Digital*.

"*We're still in the early stages of the Information Age, but the convergence of computing and telecommunications technology is rapidly transforming the way we work, live and learn. Surviving the Information Age is a practical resource for a generation still wary of powerful information technologies, written with humor, insight and a good deal of common sense. By guiding readers through the sometimes intimidating domain of information technology, this book will help them prepare for the challenges and opportunities of a networked society, giving them the understanding and confidence we'll all need to participate fully in the wired world of the new millenium."*

Jean C. Monty, President and CEO,
Nortel (Northern Telecom)

Contents

About the Author. vi

Chapter 1 Yesterday's Tomorrow. 1

Chapter 2 Would You Ride a Virtual Stimulator?. 8

Chapter 3 Do You Need to Worry About the Wired World?. 15

Chapter 4 You Must Discover Your Own Magic. 24

Chapter 5 Careers End 30

Chapter 6 What Is Holding Us Back? 41

Chapter 7 A Glance Behind the Glass 49

Chapter 8 Stupid People, or Stupid Computers? 57

Chapter 9 Who Designs This Stuff?. 65

Chapter 10 Shopping in a State of Confusion. 75

Chapter 11 The Futz Factor 84

Chapter 12 A Day in the Life of the Help Desk 94

Chapter 13 Comprehending Geekism. 104

Chapter 14 The Promise of Technology 115

Chapter 15 A Question of Trust 133

Chapter 16 Computers and Humility. 147

Chapter 17 Closing Our Minds to the Possibilities 152

Chapter 18 Accepting the Inevitability of Change 161

Chapter 19 What Does It Mean to Live in the Information Age?. . . 169

Chapter 20 The Wired World of Business. 178

Chapter 21 The Knowledgeable Organization. 187

Chapter 22 Rising Above the Crowd 196

Chapter 23 Achieving Hope 206

Credits. 215

About the Author

Jim Carroll, C.A., is on the tail end of the baby boomer revolution. He is the co-author of over 13 books, including the *Canadian Internet Handbook*. Based in Mississauga, he is a noted speaker, media personality and commentator on the future. He has been widely recognized for his unique ability to help average folks understand the economic and social implications of the emerging wired world. He and his wife, Christa, both Chartered Accountants, "retired" some years ago from the corporate rat race and now work from a "wired" home, which features a computer network extending to every room. From their electronic cocoon they assist people and organizations in understanding how to take advantage of the emerging wired world.

For more information concerning personal appearances by Jim Carroll, call:

THE NATIONAL SPEAKERS BUREAU IN CANADA
1-800-661-4110

INTERNET
http://www.nsb.com

Full details concerning speeches by Jim Carroll are also available on the World Wide Web at **http://www.jimcarroll.com**

To reach Mr. Carroll, call 905-855-2950, fax 905-855-0269 or Internet   jcarroll@jimcarroll.com

1

Yesterday's Tomorrow

Computers call up strong feelings, even for those who are not in direct contact with them. People sense the presence of something new and exciting. But they fear the machine as powerful and threatening.

Sherry Turkle, *The Second Self — Computers and the Human Spirit*
(Simon and Schuster, New York, 1984)

We of the baby boom generation are the last in the history of mankind to not have been exposed to computers since birth. Is it any wonder that we have such a unique relationship with them?

Everywhere I turn, I see baby boomers who seem to struggle on a daily basis — whether at work, at home or at play — with the ever-increasing impact of computer technology on their day-to-day lives.

I see them in their offices, silent in their frustration, as they struggle to keep up in a business world that is relentless in its march towards computer automation.

I see them in their homes, struggling to master their new home PCs, hoping all the while that they don't look too dumb in front of their children.

I listen to them talking at parties and at get-togethers, full of mixed feelings, constantly wondering if the impact of all of this new technology might be more bad than good.

I've watched them in computer stores, my heart going out to them as they try to figure out just what it is they should consider buying.

And I've met them on the Internet, listening to their messages of weariness with a technological world that sometimes seems to have gone mad.

By observing and listening to them, I think I have finally come to understand why so many people in the baby boom generation and generations before are uneasy with and sometimes freaked out by computers, the Internet and anything that has to do with what I call the "wired world." It's a story to be found throughout this book.

Let me introduce myself. I'm in my late 30s, so I'm on the tail end of the baby boom generation. In fact, you could say that I straddle two generations: I'm clearly beyond the age of the so-called Generation-X folks aged 30 and younger, but I'm young enough that I just barely qualify as an honest-to-goodness baby boomer. One generation that is wired and one that is not.

I am the co-author of over 13 popular books about the Internet, with the result that I can be seen, heard and read about quite frequently on TV, radio and in newspapers and magazines, commenting on the social and business implications of the wired world. And I've become quite a popular speaker: in the last three years I've spoken to tens of thousands of ordinary Canadians about the implications of the emerging information age as found in a world that is increasingly wired together.

I'm someone who practises what I preach. I'm quite wired myself; in fact, my wife and I work out of a wonderful home office, one that is fully equipped with all kinds of computers and communications technology. We've managed to use information technology to our advantage, with the result that we can enjoy a lifestyle and career that would be the envy of many, the best advantage of which is that my commute to work involves simply going downstairs to a large home office located on the main floor of my house, nestled in the garden amidst the trees.

In the last few years, I've become very involved in helping people and organizations understand the impact of technology on our lives. I've been successful because I am patient with people and take the attitude that if they don't "get it," it's not necessarily their fault. Because I've come to believe that it isn't.

> Computer scientists like to say that there is no danger of the machines taking over the world, as long as men can still pull the electric plug. But, according to a current joke, one scientist at least isn't so sure. For months, his machine haughtily answered every conceivable kind of question. Finally, he thought he had one that would stump it.
> "Is there a God?" he asked.
> The computer was silent for a moment. Then it answered: "Now there is."
>
> "Computers: 'Is There a God?'" *Newsweek*, January 10, 1966

I've come to appreciate that perhaps the reason the baby boom and preceding generations have such a stressful technology relationship is because they have received extremely mixed messages about these machines since day one. A journey back through yesterday's tomorrow, to news stories from the past about the future role of computers, revealed to me the roots of our distrust, a distrust that lingers to this day.

My own first encounter with a computer was in the mid-1960s at the University of Western Ontario, at the time when the Beatles had just released their *Sgt. Pepper* album, drugs were hip, the Summer of Love was in full swing, and most computers weighed in at several tons. That alone engendered concern. Back then, computers could only be found at large-scale universities, since they cost so darned much. They were of a complexity that the average person could not begin to comprehend. They were kept in separate rooms — air conditioned! — and treated with an attitude that bordered on reverence. The people who attended to them? They wore white jackets with plastic pocket protectors and spoke in a language that was incomprehensible to the vast majority of us. The machines carried an ominous name: mainframes.

The message to us was clear: *computers were special*.

In those early days, we learned that computers broke down a lot; the word "bug" quickly became part of our everyday vocabulary, sending the message that computers weren't terribly reliable. And when they did break down, they did terribly nasty things. Many of us might remember hearing oh-so-typical stories in the 1960s and 1970s about a lady, for instance, who received an electric bill for $1,000,000 or about a man who received 100,000 reminder notices from his bank because the computer broke down.

The message to us was clear: *computers were dangerous and untrustworthy*!

Computers came to represent authority at a time when youth were actively questioning the "system." Remember punch cards and the phrase "do not fold, spindle or mutilate"? Punch cards were used to collect data and to obtain information, with the result that they were the handmaiden of The Establishment. In the 1960s, at Berkeley University in California — to many, the home of the counter-cultural movement — punch cards were considered to be a symbol of oppression and were accorded an appropriate degree of disrespect. The result was that people took great joy in "folding and mutilating them," although few could figure out what spindle meant.

The message was clear: *computers were superior*, so people became rebellious, concerned that computers were taking over.

Is it any wonder why baby boomers today are stressed out about the wired world? Look at the mixed messages we received early in our lives and in our relationship with technology!

I don't think that any of us can deny that our world is on the verge of a strange, potentially wonderful but certainly terrifying new era that many call the information age. One need only look to the kids of today to realize that generations after us have accepted the computer without hesitation. And regardless of our uncertainty of what this new age might mean, I think each of us hopes to be a survivor, not a casualty.

Certainly, the world of business will continue to change as the result of all this technology, and our career survival might come to depend on our ability to adapt. So I have a simple premise: a good survival skill for any baby boomer, intent on keeping his job or in establishing opportunities in the wild new "wired economy," is to be a master of the wired world.

The purpose of this book is to give you the encouragement, motivation, and willingness to be a survivor. Surviving the information age doesn't mean that you need to know how to build a computer or that you need to know every little thing on your home PC. It does mean adopting an attitude that you can master the technology, rather than continuing to have it the other way around.

My advice? You need an attitude adjustment! That's why I've written this book. I think a lot of baby boomers need some advice on this emerging wired world, to ensure that they have the skills necessary to survive in the economy of tomorrow. This book isn't about trying to teach you how to use a computer or how to "surf the Internet," but it will help you get the right attitude and get into the right frame of mind so that you are *ready* to master the wired world of the future.

As a starting point I suggest the following:

1. Take the time to understand why you need to be a full participant in the newly emerging wired world. The fact that you've bought this book is a good start. You should be willing to accept and comprehend the possibilities that exist for personal and professional growth through the mastering of information technology, and throw away your attitudes of intimidation, confusion and concern.

   It's all too easy to fall into the trap of thinking that you don't need to master this stuff or that you simply are too dumb to "get it." It's simple to dismiss that what is happening with things involving computers, the Internet and other information technology is something that won't affect you. It's the easy way out to think that you don't need to worry about all this "stuff" because your life will go on largely as it has before.

   These are defeatist attitudes, and if you find yourself dusting off your résumé because you've become a casualty of the emerging networked economy, you'll come to realize that maybe you were wrong in your way of thinking.

2. Recognize that the wired world and the information age are not about geeky computer stuff but are about survival.

   My attitude is that we will soon see dramatic change in the business world as the result of an economy that is increasingly networked together with computer technology. Business has only just started to figure out the real potential of computer automation, and we are only just entering the "wired economy." We are in for an era of career upheaval, as our entire corporate world begins to change around us.

   The reality of the future? If you remain "unplugged," you'll be operating at a tremendous disadvantage compared to those who are "plugged in." In fact, those who are "wired" will have the good jobs, and those who are not will suffer as the future marches on.

If you are willing to recognize these truths, then I'd like to challenge you to take charge of your life by concentrating on enhancing your survival skills for the future.

2
Would You Ride a Virtual Simulator?

> *Our thoughts are traitors and make us lose the good we oft might win by fearing to attempt.*
> William Shakespeare

I'm a pretty wired individual. You could call me "plugged in." After all, take a look around my home. I have six computers, a fax machine, a laser printer, and four phone lines. I've wired them all together with a computer network that extends to every room in the house, making me perhaps one of the few people in the city who boasts a local area network in the home.

If I want to, I can take my laptop to the kitchen and do some work at the table simply by plugging into the main computer back in my home office. I also have a computer network jack beside the pool, so I can do some work out there too. After all, one has to have one's priorities right!

I'm not some dweeb, techno-nerd punk geek computer hacker; I'm just an average fellow who has mastered the wired world, with the effect that I've been able to carve out a marvelous and highly enjoyable career. I'm a survivor.

A year ago, my wife and I commissioned an addition to our suburban home to build a proper home office. We needed the extra room, since both of us now work from home. Both chartered accountants but now working to help people comprehend the impact of technology on our lives, it's fair to say that both of us have given up on the corporate rat race.

In fact, I stopped commuting to a regular job six years ago, and my wife joined me three years later, shucking off her position as comptroller for a large packaged goods company. Today? We work out of a wonderful home office that places us among the birds and squirrels, not the office towers and the clogged streets.

I put the blame for this marvelous state of affairs directly on computer technology and the wonders of telecommunications. In so doing, I wonder why so many other people in my generation and those before me remain so darned intimidated by anything that has a computer chip inside it.

After all, consider our situation: we're in touch with our clients, publisher and other business associates on a regular basis, using that marvel of the computer age known as electronic mail, or e-mail. We type all of our own letters and do our own filing — electronically. The accounting for the company is done on a PC, and a lot of the research for the books that I write is done using various computer systems. I market my services and make myself known globally through the Internet.

All this technology is the reason *why* I can work at home. And I think it's fair to say that I've mastered how to survive in the information age.

Let me reinforce an important point: we are not computer geeks nor are we techno-dweebs. We are simply two people who have discovered that the true power of technology and computer automation is that it allows people to make some pretty serious — and advantageous — lifestyle choices: while others fight it out in rush hour, we spend time with our kids. A traffic jam to us is negotiating our way through some toys scattered on the floor, which we inevitably encounter when we walk out of our home office, up the stairs, and into the rest of the house.

But what we have come to appreciate is that we're an exception and that many people in our generation, and those before us, continue to be mystified and threatened by technology at the same time that they might view it as an opportunity. That point came home to me personally when I was lucky enough to be invited to the grand opening of the first Sega Playdium in Canada, near my home in Mississauga, Ontario.

It seemed everyone was invited to the Sega Playdium that day. There were mayors and councillors, business executives, kids, parents, and babies in carriages. The place crawled with people, and everyone was encouraged to try out the "toys" — all for free. We were all provided with a credit card size piece of plastic — the payment card — which we could use to try out anything we liked.

What a place it is! It's a true hi-tech wonder. You could think of it as the ultimate arcade game facility. I'm not talking about your average run-of-the-mill TV-style video games. This place features fascinating *devices* that you actually sit on! Sega calls them "virtual simulators," and that they are: climb aboard a motorcycle, check out the screen in front of you, turn the throttle. It looks innocent enough, but moments later you're twisting and turning your body from side to side as you careen through the race course, desperately slamming yourself to one side every once in a while in order to miss a tree — or a pedestrian. Travelling too fast? You'll know it — you actually *feel* the effects when your motorcycle slams into an imaginary wall on the screen.

All the while, techno-music — throbbing at 120 beats per minute — blares through massive loudspeakers. Over the din, you can barely make out the volume of hundreds of different TVs hanging from the ceiling. Lights flash, bells ring, people scream. Noise reigns.

Within a few minutes of entering the building, I began to see a fascinating dynamic — a generation gap, it seems, applies to the world at the Sega Playdium.

First there are the kids, to me, anyone under the age of 25. They rush about, practically running from game to game, immediately trying everything out. It's almost as if they are in a race, since they all seem to be in such a hurry. They don't take the time to read the instructions for any particular attraction, nor do they study how a particular machine might operate. There seems to be no pause as they get involved with each new game; they just insert their payment card, hop on and go. Is it just me, or are these kids living in a world that is incessantly instant?

> **By the time today's preschoolers have finished their schooling, they will have had more direct experience with computers than 95% of today's adults.**
> Mark R. Lepper and James D. Milojkovic, "The 'Computer Revolution' in Education: A Research Perspective," in *Young Children and Microcomputers,* edited by Patricia F. Campbell and Greta G. Fein (Allyn & Bacon, Massachusetts, 1986)

Educators noticed this about children quite some time ago; in the book *Young Children and Microcomputers* (Allyn & Bacon, Massachusetts, 1986), the authors quoted a study from "Microcomputers and Young Children: An Interactive View," by Greta G. Fein, which said that "when faced with a new and intricate object, children will explore its salient features. Some explore it exhaustively, moving from one feature to the next, while others get hooked on one or two features, exploring those in depth before moving on to the next."

Then there are the stressed-out baby boomers and older folks. It seems most of them just stand about and watch the kids in fascination. I wonder ... is it because they are tired out, feeling the early or later effects of middle age? I don't think so; it's not a form of physical tiredness I realize, but a form of mental weariness.

To me, it quickly became obvious that many in this techno-challenged group don't rush up to one of these whiz-bang-razzle-dazzle arcade games and hop right on *because they don't understand.* Instead, they stand back and watch someone else use the machine first. They then approach the device cautiously, after first looking around to make sure no one is watching. Carefully, they read the instructions and then insert their payment card with trepidation.

A man can succeed at almost anything for which he has unlimited enthusiasm.

Charles M. Schwab

The activities at the Sega Playdium are typical of the different generational approaches that we see with technology: kids have no fear of all this marvelous new technology, while anyone older than 35 seems to be completely freaked out by what is going on!

As I stood there that day, observing, I found myself wondering why we of the baby boom generation are so confused and nervous about this crazy wired world in which we live, when the kids seem to have it figured out and deal with it with so little stress.

Think about it. Have you ever watched kids with a personal computer? They plunge right in, pounding away at the keyboard, taking just minutes to figure things out; there seems to be absolutely no fear there. I've seen kids as young as 2 use a computer mouse — with a glimmer in their eye. They know that they are in charge.

But it's an altogether different story with adults. I find that I am regularly helping out neighbours with various aspects of their new home computers, individuals who seem to be tremendously confused about every tiny aspect of the computer. I watch many adults struggle with even the simplest and most straightforward computer program — and observe them often walking away in frustration.

Adults have a lot of hang-ups about computers and everything that goes with them. The result is that many of them are not taking full advantage of the marvels of the wired world, the onrush of technology and communications capabilities that are taking us rapidly into what the media calls the information age.

Whether it's the Sega Playdium or the wired world, we know we are entering a new, strange and perhaps dangerous world and recognize that we must understand it and be part of it. Even so, we stand back, aloof, confused, nervous, afraid to hit the keyboard or hop on a virtual simulator at a place like the Playdium.

We might be using computer technology on a regular basis but perhaps not taking full advantage of the marvels the technology offers, since our unique attitudes are holding us back. We might be dabblers, staring at our fancy new home computer, but not sure where to begin, intimidated into failure by the fear of failure itself.

Whether we are novices or veterans of the world of computer technology, we must ask ourselves, why are we afraid? What has brought us to this state of being unplugged? Perhaps a sense of adventure is required, perhaps some risk must be taken. Maybe, just maybe, we should loosen up a little and approach all of this new technology as a game, not as an enemy.

Here are a few suggestions that I would like to make:

1. Learn to ride a virtual simulator — without the fear that everyone is watching what you are doing!

2. Examine the attitudes of the kids and emulate them. Spend some time watching a 2-year-old with a computer and learn from her sense of awe and wonderment. Do what she does!

3. Experiment, experiment, experiment! Kids aren't afraid to hit the buttons to see what they do and neither should you. After all, the kids don't break it easily, do they? And what's wrong if you do break it?

4. Recognize that there will never be another generation of people like ourselves; every generation from this point on will *grow up* with technology. Recognize you have a distinct disadvantage because of this and work to overcome it!

5. In order to survive, you must be a willing participant, not a casualty on the sidelines. Generate some courage, plunge right in, and be damned with what happens! As Albert Einstein said, "in the middle of difficulty lies opportunity."

6. Finally, plan for the future and realize that by mastering computer technology today, you'll one day be able to understand your grandkids, nieces and nephews.

We are in a unique situation: never before has there been, and never again will there be, a generation that has witnessed so much promise and terror at the same time from a new, emerging technology as we have with the computer.

> **The greatest discovery of my generation is that a human being can alter his life by altering his attitude of mind.**
> William James

3

Do You Need to Worry About the Wired World?

...the 1960s' future has become the 1990s' present... people now are enveloped in the revolution that was forecast in the 1960s. It's all around us!

"The revolution in the workplace: What's happening to our jobs?"
The Futurist, March/April, 1996

In the late 1890s there were some people who honestly believed that in the future it would be impossible for everyone in the United States to have a telephone. Their reasoning? A bit of simple math showed that there weren't enough young ladies age 15 to 22 to take care of telephone switchboards! And, after all, we would always need telephone switchboards!

Talk about a politically incorrect statement! Aside from the rather extreme male chauvinism in such thinking, there's an important point to be learned here: even back then, people had a tendency to think that the world around them was not going to change too much in the future. It's a trap that all too many people fall into. With so much technological change happening all around us, it's all to easy to subscribe to that most common of all human beliefs: thinking that tomorrow is going to be like today.

> **Millions of workers are being displaced in today's information revolution, causing them enormous stress and pain. We may, like the Luddites before us, rebel—or we may join the revolution and reinvent ourselves.**
> "The revolution in the workplace: What's happening to our jobs?"
> *The Futurist,* March/April, 1996

Dealing with the future is an uncomfortable topic for many people; it's much easier to simply hope that the complexities of change won't impact us. This is particularly true when it comes to technology involving computers and telecommunications: just as people in the late nineteenth century couldn't comprehend how telephone systems would evolve, many of us simply cannot comprehend what types of communication devices might be available to us 5, 10 or even 50 years from now. So we do the safe thing: we think that the world of tomorrow will be much like it is today.

It's easy to believe that the world won't change and to ignore the rapid pace of technological development. After all, in the nineteenth century there was no appreciation for the fact that we would see the emergence of giant, massive telephone switching devices that would render irrelevant the role of the telephone switchboard operator. Back then, people couldn't begin to comprehend that some 100 years later, most homes would have two or three telephones, if not more, and that some people would actually have three or four different telephone numbers: fax, business, residential, and cellular!

They couldn't begin to realize that we would have a massive global telephone system that permits us to reach any one of several hundred million people simply by punching in a few phone numbers, and that it would often cost mere pennies per minute to communicate anywhere on the globe.

> **Back in the good old days of stable economic expansion—the 1950s and 1960s—a person could choose to do something new, exciting, and innovative in life but could also choose to say, "That's not for me: I am going to play it safe in life. I am going to stay in my home town and have a nice comfortable career in a salaried job." That second choice no longer exists for the vast majority of Americans. All of us are going to be innovators and pioneers over the next 10 years whether we like it or not, and many of us don't like it.**
>
> "The revolution in the workplace: What's happening to our jobs?"
> *The Futurist,* March/April, 1996

And today we look back at them and laugh. Switchboard operators — how could they have been so blind! Might we be laughed at by future generations? Perhaps, if we don't open up our eyes to the potential impact of all this technological change that surrounds us.

Can we even begin to comprehend what is going to happen to the way we work and play, as the wired world of the future takes hold around us? We better. The reality is that we are in for an era of unprecedented change, and it will be those individuals who are willing to understand, appreciate and take advantage of the changing circumstances who will survive and prosper. Those who fail to adapt ... well, let's just say that their unwillingness to accept change will mean that they will find their own personal success to be less certain.

It's important to appreciate what is beginning to occur around us. When speaking to large groups of people, I often use the words "wired world" to describe the fact that we are entering a world in which the whole of information, ideas and knowledge possessed by mankind will one day be shared and made accessible to others around the planet through sophisticated computer and telecommunication systems, connected by massive numbers of wires. The precursor lies with us today in that system known as the Internet; in it we can see tantalizing signs of what will come, as the early foundations of the wired world are laid. But take a look around you at the explosion of new communications methods that have become available. As we leave the twentieth century and move into the year 2000, it has become clear to most people that the options available to communicate abound; the Internet, cell phones, fax machines, radio-based telephones, personal satellite dishes and other assorted technologies are becoming commonplace.

The effect of the wired world will be dramatic, but only those of us who embrace the technology will harvest its riches.

In many ways, we are on the precipice of an amazing new age, and I think our children understand that. They are full of wonder and excitement about technology and view it as a tool, a friend, that will help carry them into the future. They are busy carving out new careers and new opportunities as they explore the computer frontier around them. Adults who have consciously embraced technology take the same attitude, turning a threat into opportunity. We would do well to learn from both of them.

Looking back in time, of course, we can find ample evidence that technological change has had a massive impact on our existence. Everything from telephones to automobiles to computers has had an often significant and dislocating impact on our business and personal lives. The wired world is going to have an even more dramatic impact; there can be no doubt that we are in for an amazing new world, one involving a lot of computer and telecommunications "stuff."

> ...the really beneficial impacts of a new technology don't arise until two-thirds of the way through the transition...that moment is just ahead, in the next five to 10 years. The new integrated information technology, highly refined and matured,

> **is about to avalanche into all of our homes and workplaces, enriching and complicating daily life for everybody.**
> "The revolution in the workplace: What's happening to our jobs?"
> *The Futurist,* March/April, 1996

But gazing into a crystal ball and trying to predict what the future will look like in terms of technology is extremely difficult for anyone to do, and to be honest, nobody really knows where this wired world is headed from a technology perspective. After all, no one was able to predict the explosive growth of the Internet five years ago, just as no one was able to predict the arrival of telephone switches earlier in the twentieth century.

But the real challenge is not to predict what type of technology we might be using 5 or even 50 years hence, but to predict how our lives might change because of the emergence of the wired world. And that we can do with some degree of certainty and with conviction that the wired world will cause profound and dramatic change to our business, personal and social lives.

Although we can't blame it directly on the wired world, we can say that the broad wave of change that rippled through the last decade is but a harbinger of things to come.

Consider what happened with the recession of 1990–1991, the first "white-collar recession." We saw large-scale mergers, in which organizations joined forces to pool their efforts and combine their talents. We saw massive layoffs, as companies restructured to try to squeeze out some additional profits. The era of "re-engineering" took hold, as companies attempted to change the way they worked.

> **Most employers can carry on with fewer office workers, it seems. And productivity climbs. Indeed, 1992 alone produced a greater gain in nonmanufacturing productivity than the three previous decades combined.**
> Arno Penzias, *Harmony — Business, Technology & Life After Paperwork*
> (Harper Collins, New York, 1995)

One result? A large number of white-collar professionals found themselves on the street for the first time, victims of the so-called "corporate rationalization" of the 1990s. An explosion in the number of home-based offices occurred. Small business became the real engine of the economy, creating jobs at a frenzied pace while big business generated not much more than unemployment. Corporate joint ventures, partnerships and global business became everyday realities. The business world of the white-collar professionals changed dramatically, for the fact of the matter was that the era of the "job for life" had come to an end. People began to learn that they had to take care of themselves, since the corporate world would no longer.

The recession of the 1990s was a warning shot in a war that has not yet finished, and the negative effects on our careers have not yet ended. The business world continues to march forward with layoffs, restructuring, re-engineering and downsizing, much of which can be attributed to their ongoing success with the deployment of information technology. Reality? A lot of people have had some pretty challenging career changes and will continue to do so.

But it's not all bad. Take a look around you to find those who responded to the change of the early 1990s with enthusiasm. From my perspective, they seemed to be the folks who established a small business or began a home office. And in most of those cases, they helped ensure the success of their new venture by embracing technology; they took the time to build themselves a new future by leveraging off the power and capabilities of computer technology. Rather than viewing it simply as a threat, they turned it into an ally. There's a pretty powerful lesson there for anyone.

My exposure to the future came in 1989. Up until then, I was certainly living a charmed life. An employee of a massive global accounting firm for ten years, I knew the comforts of job security and a certain paycheque. And it was a career of excitement: from 1987 to

1989, I spent a lot of time working on a global project within the company. I was literally living the jet-set life, flying regularly to New York and Washington, with occasional trips to London, Paris and Brussels.

All of that suddenly ended in the summer of 1989, as my career undertook a dramatic and significant change three days before my marriage. That was when the firm that I worked for merged with another, a smaller firm, in Canada. By the time the dust settled, I was no longer sitting in business class on an overseas junket; I was stuck in a smallish office in a huge downtown Toronto office tower, pondering my future and dealing with people with a particularly mean brand of office politics. No longer did I visit the latest, greatest restaurant in New York. I was grabbing a quick hot dog on the streets of Toronto while trying to escape, for a few minutes at least, the latest office idiocy.

I had become a casualty of yet another corporate mega-merger, similar to so many other mergers that irrevocably changed the lives of so many people. And within a year, I decided to bail out and start my own company, working out of my home. I haven't looked back since. The first thing that I did was create the best darned home office I could, equipped with as much computing power as I could afford.

It's very scary to me that so many in my generation seem to have an innate fear, suspicion or frustration with the tools of the future. If you can't deal with the challenges of today, how the heck do you plan to survive what tomorrow is going to throw at you?

You are going through life blindfolded if you miss this fact: the business world has finally figured out that the true power of the computer revolution lies in the opportunity for ever-increasing rates of productivity and efficiency.

> **Things turn out best for people who make the best of the way things turn out.**
> John Wooden

There is no doubt that the world in which we work and play is undergoing significant change. If we open a newspaper today, we are told that we are becoming "knowledge workers," working in a world economy that is increasingly becoming "digital."

And I think that for many of us, the impact of such words is becoming much more real than abstract; it's not simply about buzzwords anymore. It's my belief that through the next decade the business world will continue to discover that the wired world will mean that companies can do business with far fewer people.

Compared to the future, the recession of the 1990s will look like child's play.

People will continue to discover that they are struggling to find an opportunity in a world that no longer values their "paper-pushing" skills. They'll discover that if they can't overcome the intimidation that they face with all of this new technology, then their lack of skills will come back to haunt them. After all, of what use is a paper-pusher in a business world that values one's ability to be a master of technology?

> **If we keep doing what we're doing, we're going to keep getting what we're getting.**
>
> Stephen Covey

As for me, the simple fact of the matter is that today I don't have a job, and haven't had one for over six years. And it's likely that I'll never have a job.

There are three primary things that I have learned since 1989 which I think you should consider:

1. You can't rely on the corporate world anymore to take care of you; you have to take care of yourself.

    This attitude will become even more important for many people as this era of unprecedented change caused by the wired world begins to take hold. It's nice and easy when you have a job, with a guaranteed paycheque and some degree of security.

Life can be awfully comfortable. But those days are coming to an end. After all, a popular saying has long held that you shouldn't wait for your ship to come in. Swim out to it.

2. A willingness to accept change, particularly the forthcoming change in the way we work, will be critical to your own personal survival.

    You can't close your eyes to what is going on around you. Survival comes from awareness, and awareness comes from observing. Observing that things aren't like they used to be, and never will be again.

3. You've got to view the threat as an opportunity. Although career changes can be pretty scary, they should be viewed as an opportunity to do something you have always wanted to do. Whether that be starting your own business, working closer to home so you can see your family more, or changing a hobby into a full-time career, maybe it's time to try it! You may be very pleasantly surprised at the support you will get from family and friends, many of whom will envy you for trying something new.

Remember these words from a fellow named Ferdinand Foch: "The most important weapon on earth is the human soul on fire." Your career, your potential, your future are being tossed into the furnace of a changing economy, so turn the challenge into an opportunity by setting your soul on fire. You've got to discover what you need to do to light it!

4

You Must Discover Your Own Magic

> *It is supremely ironic that people living in the Information Age feel more, rather than less, ignorant.*
>
> "The Information Technology Revolution,"
> *The Futurist*, July/August, 1992

If you are like most people in my generation, you've made a lot of attempts to deal with computers. You probably use one in your job one way or another; after all, recent surveys by Statistics Canada indicate that 58% of Canadians use computers at work. And there's a good chance that you have a home PC; the same surveys indicate that 41% of Canadian homes now sport such devices.

You've probably made some tentative efforts into exploring what you can do with the machine and might feel that you've mastered it. Or maybe you have learned to do a little bit with it but continue to find the whole darn thing mysterious.

> **We are born with nothing more than a fear of noise and a fear of falling. That's all. Everything else is acquired.**
>
> Peter Legge, *You Can If You Believe You Can* (Eaglet Publishing, Burnaby, B.C., 1995)

Your attitude might be that you will learn only what is absolutely necessary to do your job, or you might show your reluctance by indicating that you simply don't have the time to devote to learning more about it. You may or may not be using things like CD-ROMs, the Internet or other online services. One way or another, the fact that you are reading this book demonstrates that you think there is still something more that needs to be done.

You also probably spend some time thinking — realizing, perhaps — that the rest of the world is leaving you behind. You feel out of it and probably feel somewhat in the dark, as headlines all around you scream about the information revolution. All around you, you see a techno-elite — people who are "plugged in" — easily mastering their own computer activities while you stumble along in the dark. You're confused, bewildered and skeptical about this whole darn thing. You need some encouragement. Let me try and give you some.

What does it mean to live in the information age?

Many things. It might mean making some type of much-needed lifestyle change, or it might be doing whatever is necessary to ensure career success. It might mean that you decide to become a willing participant in the change that is occurring within your job due to technology, rather than watching warily, suspicious and nervous, from the sidelines. Or it can mean that you've developed the ability to command the resources of your computer such that you can get information about something when you need it, whether it be personal, such as information about a specific vacation spot, or business-related, such as the latest information about a specific industry.

Surviving the Information Age

Living in the information age means that you've discovered some type of magic that causes you to sit back and say, "Hey, I've done it!" Not only that, but "Hey, that was good!" And finally, that it has helped to achieve some type of positive change in your life and has given you a skill that you can somehow capitalize on later.

I've discovered all kinds of magic from the information age, and even though I've been at this for 15 years, I still sit back every once in a while and say to myself, "Wow, that was pretty amazing!"

It happened yet again while I was writing this book.

One morning I took time out from my writing to talk to the morning man of a popular Winnipeg AM radio show. One of many such calls I take during the course of a week, I ended up spending about 10 minutes talking with the chap live, on-air, about something having to do with the Internet. It was about 8:30 a.m. As I was talking with him, I thought to myself, "Gosh, that feels weird." I had noticed that while I was talking, my mouth felt like I had just received a shot from the dentist.

Maybe I slept on a funny angle, putting some pressure on my chin, I thought. It would go away. It didn't. By 9 a.m. it was feeling very weird indeed — and was getting worse. My eye had started to droop, and the entire left side of my face was tingling. A stroke, I wondered? No, couldn't be. A cold? Nope, no other symptoms involving that. A simple headache? Too complicated for that. Strange.

> **I know of no more encouraging fact than the unquestionable ability of man to elevate his life by conscious endeavor.**
>
> Henry David Thoreau

By 9:30 I knew what was happening: I figured I was coming down with a condition known as Bell's Palsy. Why? A sister and brother of mine had the condition before, and I remember what they went through. I called my sister and told her what was happening; she confirmed that it started the same way with her. It's a rapidly hitting disease that has the nasty effect of shutting down one half of your face.

I called my family doctor to set up an appointment and got one for late in the day. Curious, I was determined to find out more. So I signed on to the Internet. For me, the magic of the information age comes from my ability to gather knowledge just in time — and just when I need it — on any topic I am confronted with.

I immediately set out to learn as much as I could about Bell's Palsy. Even as the condition worsened by the hour, I was discovering sources of information from hospitals, research institutions, health care organizations and doctors from around the world about the disease: what causes it, the diagnosis, how long it would last and how to deal with it. Not to mention descriptions of the symptoms, all of which matched the ones I was feeling right at that moment.

My research continued. I soon learned that although it was a terribly distracting — and from my perspective, rather miserable — disease, it was not life-threatening. I also found information on commonly prescribed drugs and facial exercises that should be done.

Magic? And then some! I found a place sponsored by the Department of Neurology at the Massachusetts General Hospital called the Neurology Web Forum. It featured a place where people from around the world who were suffering from Bell's Palsy spent some time posting their own personal stories of what they were going through. It was as though I had walked into a room full of all kinds of people in the same state as I was! I spent an hour browsing hundreds of items that people had posted in the last several months, and started to feel some confidence, even as my condition worsened.

I also quickly observed that some con artists seemed to use the Internet to promote some rather dubious health care products related to the disease; this reminded me that an important skill in this day and age is to judge the validity of what you read.

By 5 p.m. I was in touch with five other people around the world who had come down with the disease in the previous week, forming instant online friendships that would last through the next several weeks as I coped with the disease.

I finally visited my doctor at 6 p.m. and was able to ask him some pretty blunt, pointed questions, thus turning my visit away from the typical one-way overview into a two-way conversation. I knew enough to ask the right questions, but enough not to be arrogant with my findings. As a patient, I had a better idea of how he could help me and what I could expect.

Through the next several weeks I struggled on. Aside from the tremendous support from my wife through those two weeks — another benefit of a home office — I was encouraged and cheered up by my new friends online. Eventually I recovered. And through the entire process I would sit back every once in a while and think that this must be what it means to survive in the information age. Even veterans of the information age are awed by what it can mean.

> **Many people wait for something to happen or someone to take care of them. But people who end up with the good jobs are the proactive ones who are solutions to problems, not problems themselves, who seize the initiative to do whatever is necessary, consistent with correct principles, to get the job done.**
> Stephen R. Covey, *The 7 Habits of Highly Effective People* (Simon & Schuster, New York, 1989)

What is the solution to your problem? I have only one answer: you have to commit to discovering your own magic. The information age is whatever you want it to be, and technology is simply the vehicle that will help you to get there.

Folks like myself, who have discovered our own magic online, are just like you. But we are different in that we have managed to finally do something that has given us the encouragement to plunge ahead. Everyone who works with the technology of computers struggles along, just like you do. They encounter the same pain, difficulties, anger, confusion and frustration. Until one day, they discover some type of magic in what they do, something that finally captures their attention and imagination and makes them sit back and think, "I did it!"

You've got to keep plugging away until you discover that magic. After all, the best way to survive the information age is to be a willing participant.

> **If you have tried to do something and failed, you are vastly better off than if you had tried to do nothing and succeeded.**
> Unknown

5

Careers End

...change due to technology is perhaps the most important force in economic growth in our country.

"Technology and Wealth," *Journal of the American Society of CLU & ChFC*, January, 1996

My own career experiences are similar to what many people went through with the recession and business upheaval of the 1980s and 1990s. A lot of people found themselves in circumstances that forced them to re-examine their lives and make some decisions with regard to their careers. Some responded marvelously and others did not. In my case, I've discovered a new flexibility in my attitude towards work: I find that my attitude now is that I have to continually change myself and my skills in order to keep one step ahead in the game. Since I don't have a job, I have to constantly invent one.

> **It's not what happens to you, it's what you make of it.**
>
> Anonymous

As I look around me, I see so many others in my generation and generations before who can't accept the change that is occurring all around them. To me, their attitude is chilling. Let's go back to opening night at the Sega Playdium.

After an hour or so, I found myself standing in line waiting to enter an IMAX movie presentation about a roller coaster ride. It's one of the activities an adult can partake in at the Playdium without feeling self-conscious; after all, it's dark, like a movie theatre, so there aren't a lot of people watching you. You can easily hide your intimidation in the dark.

Above the noise I heard a lady directly behind me, making the comment, with a sense of humour and awe, "Look at her." Turning, I noticed that the lady was about my age. She was nudging the fellow next to her, diverting his attention to a young girl, perhaps 6 years old, who was standing beside a "motorcycle ride." Sorry — it's called a "motorcycle virtual simulator" at the Playdium. "How does she know what to do?" the lady asked her friend. "I wouldn't know where to start. And I'm sure not going to try!"

She's intimidated, I thought to myself. Unplugged.

A few minutes later, I noticed a gentleman, perhaps in his 50s. He was in an area that had some older-style video games, similar to pinball machines. Since these games were likely not of interest to the younger generation — they couldn't compete, I suppose, with virtual reality motorcycle simulators — this area was rather quiet and deserted. The gentleman was trying to figure out one of the games. He had clearly staked out his turf, and out of the watchful eye of anyone he was going to try to figure out one of the games.

He's intimidated but determined, I surmised. Plugged in.

To me, the contrast was stark and vivid: the lady observing the young girl clearly had an attitude problem; there was no way that she was going to be able to deal with technology! Yet the gentleman showed an attitude of survival: come what may, he was going to figure it out!

When it comes to this new wired world, if you continue to react like the lady at the Sega Playdium — too intimidated by a virtual simulator to try it out — you won't survive the new wired future. You'll likely be one of the first casualties through the next decade as technology rushes in to change our business landscape, if you haven't been a casualty already.

But if you react like the gentleman — determined to understand the change that is occurring around you, demonstrated by a willingness to figure things out, you'll have a chance.

You must be willing to accept the inevitability of the change that will be fuelled by the information age. In an article in the *Journal of the American Society of CLU & ChFC* in January, 1996 titled "Technology and Wealth," the author noted that "in the Information Age, the key is knowing that there will be change, and the winner is the one who can make the right changes in the fastest possible time. Changing the fastest depends on learning the fastest and putting things into practice the fastest. Technology can cause an entire way of doing business to disappear in five years or less. However, if we keep abreast of new technology and use it to leverage ourselves and our business, we can be a part of the new wave that replaces the old."

What gets me today is this: I see too many baby boomers walk into a facility like the new Sega Playdium and freeze. It's not that they don't like video games — I don't get any major thrill from them either — but it's their attitude: their attitude is that they *can't* figure it out! They feel they are old dogs who can't learn new tricks. And in some cases, they have an even more stunning attitude: they don't *need* to learn new tricks.

There are millions of people like this, people who continue to sleepwalk their way into the future. If they don't wake up and take control of their own destiny, they'll find that the ongoing re-engineering, downsizing, job-shifting, career-destroying change that will occur around us as the wired world takes hold will have a rather dreadful and negative impact directly on them!

By understanding in general terms what is going to happen in the future, you can prepare yourself to maintain your career — and hence your income — through a period of unprecedented change.

One of the most significant changes that is occurring is that the emergence of the wired world will result in a significant change in the relationship between a business organization and its employees.

In the good old days, there was a simple rule that the world of business operated by: people lived close to the place where they worked. Having a job meant that you got up every morning, went to work, put in your seven or eight hours and went back home.

With the wired world, of course, this is no longer true: the matter of location is quickly becoming irrelevant. With the explosion of telecommunication networks, fax machines, voice mail, e-mail and other methods of communication, the fact is that the work that people do is increasingly becoming accessible to the world of business from anywhere. You can expect this trend to continue. For all the hype and hyperbole, business is truly going global and will come to rely on the skills of people wherever they might be on the planet.

> **When you become comfortable with being uncomfortable, you will no longer fear the unknown. You will always be striving to learn and develop new skills.**
>
> Jim Harris, *The Learning Paradox* (Hignell Printing, Winnipeg, Manitoba, 1996)

Back in June of 1989, I read an article in the *New York Times* entitled "Tomorrow's Company Won't Have Walls." The author did a won-

> **I am not discouraged, because every wrong attempt discarded is another step forward.**
>
> Thomas A. Edison

derful job of putting into perspective the fact that traditional forms of business were coming to an end, primarily because of the expansion of global communication capabilities. The author foresaw that the world was already becoming one in which companies were more likely to hire expertise on a part-time, as-needed basis.

His prediction? In the future, because of increasing complexity in the business world, companies would find that they would need a lot of specialized expertise. And with ever-increasing sophistication in communication capabilities, they would find that they would be able to obtain this expertise not by hiring more employees, but by accessing that expertise from contract workers or consultants who happened to make their skills available through sophisticated telecommunications technologies wherever they might be.

Two years after I read that article, which caused me to begin to think about what was happening around me with the recession of 1990–1991, *Fortune* magazine ran a cover story called "The End of the Job." The article predicted that we were entering an economy in which "jobs" are disappearing and in which people would make themselves available to companies for short-term assignments.

And by 1996, *The End of Work*, a book that focuses on the dramatic change occurring in our economy, rocketed to the top of the international best-seller lists. One of the key premises of the book? The economy of the temporary workforce is upon us.

All these articles and books centre on two themes: the ever-increasing reliance on the temporary "workforce for hire" and a reduction in the duplication of skills throughout an organization.

Over time, companies will become leaner and meaner than they are today. They will be built around a small, core group of staff responsible for keeping the business running and will obtain the rest of their needed expertise through an ongoing and ever-growing reliance on contract workers. And specialized expertise need not be duplicated. In the old days, companies may have had a human resource expert for every division and every office location. Today, they can rely on one expert, or perhaps two or three, and make that talent available to the rest of the organization through e-mail and other methods.

These changes are real and aren't science fiction. Take a look around your world, and I'm sure you can see the signs that it is beginning to happen. Fortune 500 organizations continue to shed staff at alarming rates, as the era of downsizing and rationalization continues unabated. You've either been directly affected or will be in the future.

> **In his book *Job Shift*, William Bridges (1994) coined the phrase "dejobbing" to describe this trend to non-standard employment. He says that workers are going to be more like independent business people (or one-person businesses) than conventional employees. They are likely to work for more than one client at a time and to move back and forth across organizational boundaries — being employed full-time for a period of time, then hired to do contract work, then hired to consult, and then brought back in-house (perhaps part-time this time) on a long-term assignment. He concludes that, although there will always be enormous amounts of work to do in our economy, the work will not be contained in that old familiar employment form of standard full-time, full-year jobs.**
>
> Elaine O'Reilly, Algonquin College, and Diane Alfred, Human Resources Development Canada, *Making Career Sense of Labour Market Information* (Ministry of Education, Skills and Training, Province of British Columbia, 1996)

If you think about it, the wired world is the grease that is fueling this new type of corporate organization. The reason? With the explosion of communication capabilities, organizations can go out and access the expertise and talent of any number of people around the planet. Why hire staff when you can hire a temp? If you spend a bit of time thinking about the implications of this change, you will see that through the next decade some rather remarkable changes are in store.

The Number of Full-time Jobs Will Begin to Shrink Dramatically

The era of the job for life has clearly come to an end, and the concept of the job is becoming irrelevant as well. A new way of thinking is emerging in the corporate world, built upon a reluctance to increase staff levels, with the result that we are becoming an economy of consultants who sell their skills and talents to business on an as-needed basis.

> In times like these, it is helpful to remember that there have always been times like these.
>
> Paul Harvey

It used to be that companies entered into an employer–employee relationship in order to obtain access to some type of specialized skill or knowledge. If the company needed a new marketing specialist, it went out and hired a marketing specialist. Then came the recession of the early 1990s. With the onslaught of restructuring that occurred, companies came to appreciate that it cost a heck of a lot of money to fire people, since severance packages had become quite expensive.

A new way of thinking began to occur in the corporate world, built on this logic: if we hire staff, we might have to fire them some day, particularly if we have another recession. It costs a lot of money to fire people. So why not hire people, not as staff, but on contract or as temporary workers? The role of the wired world? Guess what. A lot of those contract and temporary workers are found on the end of a telecommunications line.

Companies Will Hire the Best Talent They Can, Regardless of Where That Person Might Be

In the wired world, the only thing that counts is knowledge. If the knowledge is accessible from anywhere in the world, then companies will find themselves in the position of being able to choose the best talent and expertise they need to do a particular job from a group of global, skilled consultants.

The impact? A new era of career competitiveness is about to unfold as a number of highly skilled workers sell their capabilities and talents to a global audience of business organizations. The result? Marginal performance is no longer going to be good enough: in the new dog-eat-dog world of networked business, the old rule that those with the best skills and capabilities will be in the greatest demand will be even more true than it is today.

Lifestyle Choice Will Come to Dominate Career Decisions

Because they can supply their skills from anywhere through the tools of the wired world, this elite group of individuals will call the shots. They will make lifestyle decisions that will let them service their national and global client base from a *rural electronic cottage*, thus enjoying the fruits of the wired economy, at the same time watching their children grow up. A new era of career decisions based upon lifestyle choices is upon us. As we enter an economy in which location doesn't matter, the natural result is that more people will choose to work from the places they *want to*, rather than where they *have to*.

> **Let us not look back in anger, nor forward in fear, but around in awareness.**
> James Thurber

Our Actual Work Location Won't Matter

You can enhance your future career and job opportunities by adapting your skills so that they are marketable and accessible via the wired world. That simple rule, people lived close to the place where they worked, that I mentioned earlier is clearly and unequivocally changing as a result of the wired world, since you don't need to be near your job in order to do the work!

On the other hand, we might consider that the rule hasn't changed: people who have mastered the technology that lets them provide their skills to others, wherever they might be, live close to the place where they work — online!

The matter of location is quickly becoming irrelevant, with the explosion of telecommunication networks, fax machines, voice mail, e-mail and other methods of communication. The office of the future will look like your bedroom — because it will be.

As companies begin to rely more and more on outside expertise, the number of core employees required will continue to decrease. The impact on downtown urban areas will be dramatic. There will be fewer people working in office towers. The real estate industry has a phrase for this: "see through buildings." That's because they will be.

Guess what — the work force of the twenty-first century wears sweatpants, not suits, since they shop at Wal-Mart, not Hugo Boss, for their day-to-day work attire. And while downtown real estate will suffer, the home improvements industry will expand, as people build a more comfortable home office environment.

If you really want to know what is happening in the world around us, talk to your letter carrier. She will tell you that her pack is getting heavier, year after year, because of the number of people working at home. Visit a local photocopy or office supply store at 10 in the morning, and you'll find a variety of semi-scruffy professionals loading up on supplies or getting some copies made.

Today, 41% of Canadians have home computers, according to Statistics Canada. Not all of them are used solely for games and homework; an increasing number sit in the home office, tools with which the new home-based workforce is meeting the challenge of the changing business world.

You can ensure you are a survivor by understanding what it takes to build, manage and work in a home office and by getting into the wired state of mind.

> **The ultimate measure of a man is not where he stands in moments of comfort, but where he stands at times of challenge and controversy.**
>
> Martin Luther King Jr.

A Generational Battle For Economic Control and Survival Is Upon Us

It won't be easy. Our economic systems are increasingly characterized by baby boomers and the older generation, comfortable in their unchanging ways and who are now faced with a new, wired and technically sophisticated Generation-X. Increasingly, economic survival is dependent upon mastery of technology, and it should be obvious who has the upper hand in this game!

Change in your life will be constant, ongoing and never-ending, particularly so with the wired world. There are a few things you must do to survive:

1. You must refuse to be intimidated by technology and the change that it represents. Adopt the attitude of the gentleman at the Sega Playdium: try something out!

2. You must accept that your ability to participate in the wired world is going to have a dramatic impact on your potential for success.

3. Accept that some of the best economic, social and political minds of the day are predicting that a unique and profound era of career upheaval will soon be upon us.

4. Accept that change is real, ongoing and that this unique thing called the wired world is going to lead to even more change.

5. Always remember that a defeatist attitude is a direct threat to your well-being!

Don't be like a deer caught in the headlights of an approaching car, frozen and unable to comprehend the onrushing danger. Accept it, comprehend it, challenge it and win.

The fundamental message...is that technology changes more rapidly than predicted, but people change more slowly. Given new technology, people tend to do the same old thing they were doing before — just a little cheaper and faster. It takes people a long time to find new applications for new technology.

Edward Yourdon, *Decline and Fall of the American Programmer* (Prentice Hall, Englewood Cliffs, New Jersey, 1992)

6

What Is Holding Us Back?

Logizomechanophobia — the fear of computers.
Sanford B. Weinberg and Mark Lawrence Fuerst, *Computer Phobia — How to Slay the Dragon of Computer Fear* (Banbury Books, Wayne, Pennsylvania, 1984)

When I started doing research for this book, I set out to locate some news articles from the 1950s and 1960s about computing technology. In doing so, I made a fascinating discovery: up until about 1963, computers weren't listed under the word "computer" in the index. Instead, they were listed under the topic "calculating machines."

The roots of our relationship with these machines are such that early on, we clearly classified them as devices that were to be used for number crunching. So whether we dabble with them, avoid them altogether or think we have mastered them, we of the baby boom generation suffer from the ingrained understanding that computers are "calculating machines."

> **Always do what you are afraid to do.**
>
> Ralph Waldo Emerson

Let's get right down to it. There are many different types of people on this planet. There are creative individuals and individuals who are not creative. Some excel in the arts, whether music, writing, drawing or painting, and there are some who probably failed finger painting in kindergarten (like me; I don't have an artistic bone in my body).

And there are those who excelled in math in their youth and those who didn't. Face it: the "mathies," folks who took physics and engineering and who delighted in complex calculus courses, were drawn to computer technology in the 1950s and 1960s, because at that time computers were considered to be "calculating machines."

For the rest of us, well, the mere thought of mathematics engendered a feeling of peril, so our nature didn't naturally draw us to the world of computers. After all, that was a world for the math-geeks, and computers were "giant brains" that excelled at mathematics.

This was particularly so before the 1990s. In the book *Computer Phobia — How to Slay the Dragon of Computer Fear* (Banbury Books, Wayne, Pennsylvania, 1984), authors Sanford B. Weinberg and Mark Lawrence Fuerst noted that "in the course of our studies, we've discovered…factors…closely related to computerphobia. The first is an anxiety about having to do math. Many people find computers threatening because they hear tales of "number-crunching" computers and remember that they themselves weren't good at math in school. But as you'll soon see, very little computer work really involves mathematics."

The relationship with computers in your youth might have been straightforward: computers did their thing, you did yours, and you didn't really have to worry about them. Then somebody changed the equation. Blame the folks who invented the personal computer and the computer chip. Suddenly, computers started to become much more significant in our day-to-day lives. Offices started to purchase them. People started to buy them for homes. Friends and relatives started using them.

They were appearing everywhere! "Wait a moment!" you began to think. "I had no interest in them back then, so why am I forced into dealing with these machines today?" After all, they're for the mathies, and you're not one of *those* people!

It's different for kids today. They don't suffer from the problem of automatically associating computers with math. They view computers entirely differently than we do and have never been exposed to the line of thinking that computers are "calculating machines." To them, computers do all kinds of things, so both the mathies and non-mathies are drawn to them. The result? They don't suffer from the stress that we do as a result of dealing with computers, making us unique in our attitudes towards computer technology.

> **A fascinating insight into children's perceptions of computers was revealed on the American youngster's programme *Sesame Street*. A teacher asks a group of four-year-olds a simple question — what is a computer? The answers? "It's for drawing...I use it to do designs...It's for helping you to learn to read...It's for playing games."**
> Jon Palfreman and Doron Swade, *The Dream Machine — Exploring the Computer Age* (BBC Books, London, 1991)

The fact that our generation overlaps the generation that saw the birth of computing technology — and hence viewed computers as math machines — means that our perspective of the machine is entirely different from that of our children. And it's that type of thinking that has resulted in some of the pretty unique fears and attitudes that we have related to computing technology. What are some of those attitudes? Listening to people, I hear all kinds:

"I'm gonna break it!"

I'm always teasing my neighbours that they are jinxed; every time they touch a computer something goes wrong. I think they believe it, and many other people I've met seem convinced that Murphy's Law applies to their use of a computer.

> **Some people joke that if they touch a computer, "it's going to blow up." In 1986, the *New York Times* reported that "...two owners of Compaq Portable II computers were rudely surprised recently when their machines simply blew up. The problem, said Jeff Stives, a spokesman for the Houston-based company, arose when service technicians improperly rewired the battery circuits on the computers' main circuit boards. Compaq engineers managed to blow up another computer in the tests, thus confirming the problem."**
>
> **It's expected that this problem mostly doesn't exist anymore!**
> Seen on the Internet

It's almost as if we think that if we touch a computer, we're going to do something wrong that will cause some damage! Our experiences have taught us that all too often, we can only do something wrong if we try something out, which certainly doesn't encourage us to try anything new!

"I'm gonna look dumb!"

Every once in a while I have a dream that I am back in school and about to take an exam. I wake up, terrified, and then realize that I was dreaming. The world of technology and the wired world impose that same sense of dread upon many of us; it's a terrible thing to be middle-aged and have to admit that we don't get it! The simple reality is that many people simply don't like to appear as if they aren't knowledgeable about something, particularly at this point in life when we feel we have mastered most things. We finally believe that we can stop learning and then this new thing comes along. It's frustrating to be sent to the back of the class!

> **Overthrowing the dominance of the keyboard is believed to be a key factor in opening up the knowledge bottleneck. Many people just do not like computers. Typing on keyboards is not how they are used to communicating.**
> Ronald D. Rotstein, *The Future — Trends and Developments Through the 21st Century* (a Lyle Stuart book published by Carol Publishing Group, New Jersey, 1990)

"I am dumb!"

Of course, it's all a very frustrating experience, trying to deal with these devices. We'll see that throughout this book.

You've probably experienced this: after you finally get up your courage to try something new with a computer, it doesn't work. Then, as soon as you call someone for help, it *does* work. Sheepishly you sink back in your chair and say in a small voice, "It didn't do that a moment ago." Then, to add insult to injury, as soon as your helper goes away, it stops working again!

Sometimes it seems as if these machines are possessed! Of course we know that they are not, but we must wonder. *The Weekly World News*, what many refer to as a "rag" full of sensationalized news stories, reported in 1987 the strange case of a computer that was possessed! A bank in Valpariso, Chile, installed $7.3 million worth of computer equipment, including 13 terminals. One of these computers was, over time, used by three different people — each of whom died shortly after using the machine. A workman asked to carry away the computer refused to do so, and at one point, the bank considered performing an exorcism!

"I'm not in control"

In the early days of computing, many business organizations tried to get the Chief Executive Officer — usually the President — to use a computer. Many of these efforts failed, for one simple reason: the CEO believed that he or she just simply couldn't be seen using a computer keyboard!

> Another awkward situation the personal computer is helping to break down is that old executive suite syndrome known as keyboard phobia. The affliction seems to be the result of two things: the feeling that typing (keyboarding is the euphemism) is secretarial work, and the fact that most executives never learned how to type.
>
> A. Richard Immel, "The Automated Office: Myth Versus Reality," in *The Information Technology Revolution*, edited by Tom Forester (MIT Press, Cambridge, Massachusetts, 1985)

Why? The perception of control. Face it. When someone sits down at a computer keyboard and he doesn't know what he is doing, he is no longer in control. How can the CEO of an organization be seen in such a position! There is a status issue at work as well; some of them simply don't want to be seen keyboarding, since that's a "secretarial thing," a darned silly attitude in this age of technology.

By middle age, most of us are in control of most things in our lives. It's frustrating — and nerve-wracking — to have to deal with something new that doesn't give us the same degree of control. And it's a very unique situation, this loss of control, given that this is one area where our kids are more competent than we are (another is roller blading). I know a lot of parents who are awed — and sometimes terrified — by what their children can do with a computer, which only enhances the feeling of loss of control.

"I don't have time!"

How can a soccer mom possibly find the time to learn! How can a hockey coach dad learn to use a computer? For that matter, where can you find the time to read this book? In this era of the two-income, two-career, busy family, time is a serious and important challenge. Where can we possibly find the time to learn everything that is necessary? This, I suppose, is perhaps the biggest challenge. But given the growing importance of the skill, can we afford to ignore it?

> **An expert is a man who has made all the mistakes which can be made.**
>
> Niels Bohr

"I'm not convinced I need to!"

Finally, some people remain convinced that computer technology is not something that they need to master. This is one attitude that I simply cannot fathom.

Slowly many people are being convinced that they must take part; the growth in the purchase of home computers demonstrates that fact. Obviously, many people are buying them to upgrade their skills. Yet many of those computers sit in those homes, unplugged, unloved, unused, because of our fears and our attitudes and because of our upbringing that computers are calculating machines.

> In 1987, a fellow named Michael Case of Passaic Township, New Jersey, was arrested for firing eight shots at his IBM home computer. When questioned by police, he indicated that he was angry at the computer — and didn't understand why he couldn't shoot his own computer in his own home.
> Seen on the Internet

However, another fact remains paramount: an overwhelming number of those people who have plunged ahead and overcome their fears with technology often comment on how easy it really was. The thing I have learned is that you can't fear the technology, but you should fear your attitudes. Here are some of the principles that I've used over the years:

1. Find out what is causing your mental block and face it head-on. Logizomechanophobia — the fear of computer technology — is a real and recognized type of fear. There are psychologists and scientists who study this affliction. Recognize fear for what it is; it's the first step to overcoming it!

2. Deliberately set out to learn more. Recognize that ignorance breeds fear and that if you purposely decide not to learn more about what is happening with the technology world around you, then you are doing nothing to overcome your basic fears of technology.

3. Never hesitate to ask someone for help; they've been there before! If we are made to feel dumb or believe that we are stupid when it comes to technology, we won't ask for help. But we should never hesitate. After all, there are a lot of folks in the

same boat! This means that it's OK to swallow your pride, admit that you don't get it and eat some humble pie. Remember the Chinese proverb, "He who asks is a fool for five minutes, but he who does not ask remains a fool forever."

4. As bad as things might be, keep in mind that it is probably illegal for you to shoot your computer. Heck, being in jail will probably do more damage to your career potential than any change brought on by the wired world!

7

A Glance Behind the Glass

The notion that computers are slowly taking over man and man's world inspires almost as many cartoons these days as the man-girl-desert island situation of years past. In one recent version a tousle haired scientist is sitting in a glass case above a massive computer. Below him a printed sign reads: "In case of emergency, break glass."

"The Big Whir: Computers Spin Problems and Profits," *Newsweek*, October 21, 1963

I don't have many memories of being 8 years old; you probably don't either! But one vivid memory for me is when my dad took me to an open house at the University of Western Ontario, probably in 1967. When we walked into one particular room at the university, I was instantly awestruck.

The image is still crystal clear to me today. The room contained some big typewriter-like machines, teletypes, I think they were called, that churned out paper from large rolls. There must have been 20 or 30 of them. They were noisy, with keys pounding, letters clacking and bells ringing. Important — and serious — young men and women stood around ready to offer help. There were maybe 50 people in the room.

My Dad and I waited a minute or two; it seemed much longer. I was so curious and tried to watch over some shoulders to see what people were doing. Finally, it was our turn. We stood next to the machine, and someone standing beside us pressed a button to show us how to start. The machine clattered to life:

```
Do you want to play:
1. Tic-tac-toe
2. Checkers
3. Chess
```

Being a chess buff I thought this was really neat. "What do I do?" I asked my dad. He showed me, by pressing "3" and by pressing a little button called "Enter." The machine started to clatter again.

```
Do you want to be
1. Black
or
2. White.
```

White, I thought. So I pressed "2" and looked for the "Enter" button. There it was. I pressed it. I was getting the hang of it.

```
Your move.
```

Thus began a relationship that has lasted to this day.

> **Personally, I rather look forward to a computer program winning the world chess championship. Humanity needs a lesson in humility.**
> Richard Dawkings

By growing up in the 1950s and 1960s, all of us have come to live in an era in which computer technology has undergone dramatic and fascinating change. After all, the early computers that we were exposed to are nothing like the small and friendly machines that we encounter today.

When we first started hearing about computers, they were usually massive machines called mainframes, with imposing names such as MARK I, ENIAC, UNIVAC and System/360. They were programmed in languages like FORTRAN, COBOL and BASIC. They were most often characterized by whirring tape drives and large steel cabinets with lots of flashing lights.

> **Our early introductions to the complexities of the "mainframe" helped to shape our attitudes. For example, we often encountered statements in books and magazines that focused on the sheer size of the machine:**
>
> **"In physical terms ENIAC was a monster. It was almost 100 feet long, 8 feet high, 3 feet deep and weighed thirty tons. It contained 18,000 tubes, 70,000 resistors, 10,000 capacitors, 6,000 switches, 1,500 relays and cost a little under $500,000 — well over budget."**
>
> Jon Palfreman and Doron Swade, *The Dream Machine — Exploring the Computer Age* (BBC Books, London, 1991)

Everything about them was mysterious and overwhelming. Our impressions were forged in an environment in which we could never really get near the machines themselves; after all, they were locked away in special rooms, attended to by a priesthood of computer specialists outfitted in white lab coats. Our only interaction with them came through the punch card or teletype terminal. And unlike the chess game, there was often nothing friendly about it: everything you did involved a special form of computer geek-speak.

The computer fraternity demanded respect and awe, and the computer industry itself fostered a special, reverent view of the technology. People specializing in the computer field worked in the field of "electronic data processing" and were referred to as "computer scientists." It was science, it was magic, and for most of us, incomprehensible.

News stories at the time always seemed to focus on "yet another breathtaking computer development," causing, I suppose, a bit of a ho-hum attitude with respect to technological advances that paralleled our boredom with walking on the moon after it had been done once or twice. We were on the edge of something important, we were told, and we had better pay attention! If we peeked behind the glass in the computer room, we could see the future, intimidating and confusing at the same time that it inspired awe.

At some point, we were forced to deal with computers a little bit more, even if we didn't want to. Credit card bills were computerized first. Then our bank statements. Soon the airlines, car rental companies and retail stores followed suit. Computerization was sprouting everywhere. When we had a chance to work with them, our experiences were often more baffling than reassuring.

> The first exposure that many people had to computers occurred with the 1952 presidential election, when CBS used a computer to help predict the outcome of the nationwide vote. The story is typical of the attitude found as early as the 1950s, that computers were somehow smarter and more intelligent than people.
> "...UNIVAC did have enough data to make a prediction. Just before CBS went on the air UNIVAC had predicted that Eisenhower would win by a landslide. The problem was that no one believed it because all the polls had said this was a tight race. Eckert was told to reprogram the computer, to come up with a 'more reasonable' estimate....When it emerged that UNIVAC had been right all along CBS had to come clean....Headlines the next day ranged from 'Machine Makes Monkey Out of Man' to 'Big Electronic Gadget Proves Machines Smarter Than Men'."
>
> Jon Palfreman and Doron Swade, *The Dream Machine — Exploring the Computer Age* (BBC Books, London, 1991)

For some of us, our involvement came in the form of a computer course. Mine took place on the campus of Dalhousie University in 1976, and my experiences were probably typical of many at the time.

It was the era before the emergence of the personal computer. At the time, I was taking a Bachelor of Commerce degree, and since computers were beginning to play a major role in the world of business, we were expected to learn more about them.

The course was designed by the computer science department of the university, even though it was intended for business students. It was a strange course; to this day, I cannot comprehend why we were forced to learn how computers worked, rather than taking a look at how they might be used in business. For some reason, the priests and priestesses of the computer revolution decided that I, a simple human, should learn the special nuances of their religion.

So I had to learn to do addition and subtraction using "hexadecimal notation" and spent time trying to comprehend the nature of binary numbering schemes. I was expected to learn the components of the computer: disk drives, tape readers, memory units, input and output units, CPU, RAM, ROM, down to the smallest details of the machine. The course textbook contained colourful little pictures of the details of a computer, just like a book about dump trucks for 3-year-olds contains colourful little pictures of different dump trucks.

Once we had all of these details, it came time for me to "learn how to use the computer." You see, the priests and priestesses of the computer science department decided, in their wisdom, that I and my business school peers should learn the hallowed, mystical language of the computer.

So it was that we were then forced to learn the language called BASIC. Once we had sputtered our way through that, we were expected to master something called COBOL. And if we made it through that, we would get the extra special treat of learning RPG! We spent our time trying to figure out these new "languages" in the local pub, finding that to be the best environment to deal with this new and strange world. After all, it was far better than time spent near the mainframe itself!

> **A college education never hurt anybody who was willing to learn after he got it.**
>
> Author unknown

Why did they insist on teaching us this way? It simply didn't make sense. Yet the manner in which I was introduced to computers paralleled the experience of many millions more in the 1960s, 1970s and 1980s. At one time or another, anyone who took a computer course, "computer science," as it was then called, had to learn how to write computer programs. They didn't really get a course about the impact of computers or learn about what they could do; they were expected to learn how they could do it.

All of us were expected, in effect, to learn all about the components of the engine in our car in order to learn how to drive. This type of exposure to computer technology wasn't restricted to computer courses. From their inception, much of the coverage of computer technology in magazines and newspapers focused on "how" they worked, rather than "what" they were good for.

Consider, for example, *Reader's Digest*. It fell into this trap in 1971 with its article "It's Here — The Computer Revolution." The publication, which prides itself on its ability to print friendly, human-interest stories that are readable by everyone, felt it necessary to explain to the general public how computers work. The article spoke about "binary code" and "switches" grouped into units. Binary code! In *Reader's Digest*!

> **For most computers in use today, the data are rendered into the so-called binary code, in which any number, or letter of the alphabet, can be expressed in terms of just two digits, 0 and 1. (For example, the binary equivalents of the decimal numbers one through ten are: 1, 10, 11, 100, 101, 110, 111, 1000, 1001, and 1010.) Inside the machine those binary digits — 0 and 1 — are represented by switches that may be either off (for 0) or on (for 1). The machine, in effect, consists of hundreds of tiny switches grouped into five units: Input. Storage. Control. Processing. Output.**
>
> Peter T. White, "It's Here — The Computer Revolution," condensed from *National Geographic*, *Reader's Digest*, 1971

Is it any wonder that those of us who didn't naturally gravitate to computers as a career option early on in our student days didn't take kindly to being force-fed information about how the machines work?

Perhaps it was the method of teaching that helped to engender in us a suspicion of computer technology that lingers with us to this day.

Ask yourself these questions: at some time during the last 20 or 30 years, did you encounter an article such as the one above in *Reader's Digest*? Did you have to take a computer course that focused on trying to teach you an actual honest-to-goodness computer programming language? Did you have one experience — or several — with computers and technology that was less than enlightening and closer to frustrating?

Given the way that the field has evolved over the last 30 years, the answer to at least one of these questions is likely to be yes. And maybe that's one reason why you have the attitudes towards technology that you do. It was the essence of the mainframe — dark, mysterious, overwhelming — that shaped the perceptions that are with us still.

The past is important, but it is not nearly as important to your present as is the way you see your future.

Dr. Tony Campolo

It was the fact that we lived in a unique transition period that helped to shape our attitudes — and our fears — all of which might be holding us back today. Yet even in today's world of better, easier-to-use computers, our old experiences might be shaping our willingness to adapt.

1. Don't let the past hold you back from the future. Think about your first experience with computers: was it like my own? If it was, think about this: kids today rarely see a mainframe. The result is that they have no preconceived notions about technolo-

gy, but you likely do. Toss out your old experiences, and be willing to recognize that things today are quite different from the way they were in the past!

2. Did you take a computer course that involved learning how to program a computer or that examined other esoteric stuff? Take a look through the newspaper today, and you can probably find all kinds of computer courses that teach a specific "something" rather than "how computers work."

The computer industry has come a long way in the last 30 years, finally coming to recognize that you don't have to teach people how the machines do what they do in order to effectively use them. If you previously had a bad experience, don't necessarily hold that as an indication of the way it will be in the future.

8

Stupid People, or Stupid Computers?

> *The important point to remember, particularly for a newcomer to the PC, is this: when something seems to have gone wrong, it is just as likely that you did exactly what you were told to do (or what seemed perfectly sensible to do) as it is that you failed to follow instructions.*
>
> Things the Manual Never Told You, IBM PC edition, compiled by The Boston Computer Society, edited by Jack McGrath
> (Addison-Wesley Longman Inc., Boston, 1985)

Certainly the fact that we grew up in an era that saw remarkable change has helped to shape our attitudes towards computer technology and has contributed to the reluctance that we still hold today. But it's not just history that has proven to be our enemy; when it comes right down to it, this technology simply has not been easy to use. Even today, much of the interaction that you might have with a computer or something like the Internet will prove to be a less than exciting experience.

When you sit back and read a new book, watch a movie or listen to a new CD, you most often end up enjoying it; it's a pleasant experience. Not so with computers and the wired world. The reason? The computer industry itself has, until recently, done little to make your interaction with their products a fun and enjoyable experience. In fact, I find that the attitude is such that you are often made to feel like a complete, hopeless idiot every step of the way. If you can't figure it out, you must be some kind of an idiot, right?

Is that the way you feel about computers and the wired world? Don't! I've become convinced that when it comes to mastering this technology, it isn't necessarily you and I who are the problem; it's computers, the computer industry and everything else.

> **In most cases…the problem is in the design of the user interface, but many software developers make the implicit assumption that an even larger part of the problem is that the users are somehow mentally deficient.**
> Edward Yourdon, *Decline and Fall of the American Programmer* (Prentice Hall, New Jersey, 1992)

One of the things I decided to do in 1982 when I first started to learn how to use a computer was to build a computer file containing information about all my LPs, several hundred of them. I figured that doing this would be a good learning experience, even if it was kind of a dumb idea. So one day during my lunch hour, I went and bought a program called dBase; from what I had read, this was the best thing to use to "build a database." Walking home, I imagined myself quickly mastering the art of information management on the PC.

> **While most of today's "high-quality" products work exactly as their designers intended, many of their features baffle the average user.**
> Arno Penzias, *Harmony — Business, Technology & Life After Paperwork* (Harper Collins Publishers, New York, 1995)

That night, I made a quick dinner, fired up my new home computer and started the program. This is what I got:

```
dBase Version II. Copyright Ashton Tate 1982.
```

It sat there, blinking at me, with this one simple little dot on the screen. That's it! One simple little dot. Flashing at me. Talk about a friendly introduction!

I looked around for the manual, but then realized that I had left it at work. What the heck do I do now, I thought? I typed "help." Screens full of unintelligible instructions whizzed by. I didn't even know how to stop them! The next day, I made sure that I had the manual before I left for home so that I could study it later, but then I was as lost as ever! My first foray into the world of computers wasn't turning out to be too successful. I felt the pangs of computer disillusionment for the first time. Solution? I went out and bought a book. I studied the program for quite some time. Eventually, I struggled my way through and figured out how to "build a database." My perseverance won out over the computer, my formidable opponent.

Of course, since then, things have come a long way. We are told that computers are easier than ever to use, and that it's simple and straightforward to get plugged in and go. But statistics tell us that vast numbers of Canadians remain intimidated by the mere thought of computers or the wired world or things like the Internet. Clearly something doesn't jive.

All around me, I see many people who are still struggling with anything and everything computer-related. It seems every radio and television host who has interviewed me remains stressed by the concept of the keyboard. Friends, neighbours, acquaintances, business associates and people who attend my speeches — whoever they are, I see people terrorized by the wired world.

And I think another important reason, in addition to history and attitude, is because computers and technology and telecommunications — all the accoutrements of the information age — remain formidable opponents. Things have come a long way since 1982: you don't get many programs that just stare at you with a simple dot, but even so, it's a complex and confusing world. The reality? Even today, it's you versus the computer, and you don't stand much of a chance if you don't develop the attitude that you want to win.

Arrogance Has Long Been a Problem in the Industry

Part of the problem stems from the sheer arrogance that surrounds anything having to do with computers and technology. The attitude of many people who have mastered computers — regular folks and individuals within the computer industry itself — seems to be that if you can't figure it out, then you must be some kind of an idiot! An attitude so pervasive that many think that you must have some type of mental deficiency if you can't sit down at a new computer or brand new computer program and comprehend it within a matter of minutes.

We seem to be suffering from an attitude that is so extreme that I'd be willing to call it absolute and complete arrogance. The attitude has the effect that we have become so scared of this technology that we are too nervous to try anything new, afraid to ask for help, for fear that we might end up looking like helpless, stupid human beings.

I came to realize the nature of the problem one day, when one of my

If the automobile had followed the same development cycle as the computer, a Rolls-Royce would today cost $100, get a million miles to the gallon, and explode once a year, killing everyone inside.

Robert X. Cringely

neighbours, who had recently begun to use the Internet, called me with a question.

"I can't get on the system," she said. I asked a few questions about what happened, then decided to take a run over to have a look, since I really wasn't sure what was wrong. Within a few seconds, I discovered what had happened; one of those typical small somethings that was preventing her from accomplishing what she set out to do. No big deal. But I discovered that she had had the problem since Friday, four days earlier.

"I didn't want to call you," she said. "I thought I would look kinda dumb."

Is this you? Do you hold back from asking other people for help, because you think you might look dumb? What is it, I thought at the time, that makes someone like my neighbour so nervous of calling someone else with a question?

I am sure the same neighbour would not hesitate to call me with a question if her lawn mower broke, or if she needed some help figuring out how their new pool heater worked, or if there were any number of other household problems. But because computers are involved, she is intimidated. So much so, that she refrains from asking anyone for help, because she doesn't want to look dumb. She's been scared into a submission of silence and, sadly, is like many millions of other people out there. Including, perhaps, you.

The Unreality of Computers

But the problem isn't with the computer user. Consider what you are up against. Imagine placing a long distance telephone call, only to be told by a voice on your telephone: "Illegal instruction — opcode 407. Resegment number parsing error, execute again."

It doesn't happen, does it? Instead, the telephone company uses a simple human language message, advising you that "the number you have dialed is not valid. Please hang up and try your call again." Simple, pleasant, right to the point — and understandable. Spoken in what we might call "human language."

Contrast this with computers. When something goes wrong on a computer, things get weird. Take a program like Windows 95, one of the most popular computer programs on the planet. While writing this chapter, it "crashed," something that this program seems to do on an ever-frequent basis. What did it tell me? A box appeared in the middle of the screen:

```
Word Has Executed an Invalid Instruction
This Program Has Terminated
```

A little button called "Details" was there, and so I pressed it. This is what I got:

```
Invalid Segment Offset 3E 2Y 17
0A3B17
```

Who writes this stuff? What planet are they from? Why do they work so hard to make it so unintelligible? Why can't they put up a box that says something like:

```
This program couldn't or didn't do what
you wanted it to. There could be any
number of reasons why. I'm sorry.
Please don't be stressed about it; I'm a
computer, and I occasionally break down.
```

That's why I like the Macintosh computer; at least it has a sense of humour about things. When something goes wrong, it puts up a little box with a picture of a bomb! That is certainly a lot easier to deal with than the gibberish I get from my "state-of-the-art" Windows 95 software.

Is it any wonder why you, and so many other people in our generation, might be holding back from participating in the information age?

The problem isn't that you are stupid, or that you don't have the smarts necessary to master the technology; it is that you are never *encouraged* to charge forward. It's almost as if computers have been designed to hit you on the head with some difficult, incomprehensible instruction, message or statement that sets you back every time you use it or attempt to learn something new. So probably the best piece of advice I can give you, whether you are a computer novice or an experienced computer user, is this: it is not your fault!

> **...we have come to depend on things that make us feel stupid. And a high-tech education doesn't provide relief from this dilemma.**
> Arno Penzias, *Harmony — Business, Technology & Life After Paperwork*
> (Harper Collins Publishers, New York, 1995)

Regardless of all the wonderful technical advances that have been made, the sad reality is that computers still remain a tremendously confusing and nerve-wracking challenge for many people. And you shouldn't feel bad about it! My suggestions are simple:

1. Accept that perhaps you are not the one at fault. This is a good first step in overcoming the intimidation factor you might have with the continued onrush of new technology.

   The computer revolution is more of a confusion revolution. From my perspective, I think that, across the land, a lot of people from our generation struggle day in and day out to get the darn things to do what they want them to — silently gnashing their teeth in frustration as they do so.

2. Accept that you are not dumb; you are faced with mastering something that has been developed by an industry that has long had a hostile attitude towards non-technical specialists.

3. One of the first things you must do once you make the conscious decision to survive and thrive in the wired world is to *change your attitude*. Don't feel bad if you are struggling to simply understand what is going on and what it is all about. As Eleanor Roosevelt said, "No one can make you feel inferior without your consent."

4. Recognize as well that there are plenty of people in the same boat as you. "Not getting it" isn't an aberration; in fact, it's quite common. "Computer elitism," the need to pretend that one "gets it," is so rampant that no one is prepared to admit that he is often as confused as you are.

Don't ever, ever hold back from asking someone for help because you think you are dumb, because most likely, you aren't!

> **People are failures, not because they are stupid, but because they are not sufficiently impassioned.**
> Bert Struthers

9

Who Designs This Stuff?

> *Humans...do not always behave clumsily. Humans do not always err. But they do when the things they use are badly conceived and designed.*
>
> Donald A. Norman, *The Design of Everyday Things* (Bantam Doubleday Dell Publishing, New York, 1988)

When you've been involved with computers for a long time, you inevitably end up as the one people call when they need help. Mostly you provide this help, but end up doing it with one of two attitudes: either you think the people you are helping mysteriously lose some precious brain cells as soon as they sit down at a keyboard, or you think these people are just fine and there could be something fundamentally wrong with the design of computer technology and software.

I always take the latter approach. It's a diplomatic way of keeping friends.

One day, my neighbour called me again. I had been encouraging her and her husband to explore the wonders of the Internet, so one day on her own, she had finally decided to "surf the Web," the phrase used when someone decides to explore the area of the Internet known as the World Wide Web. She was trying to find information about some real estate properties in a certain city in the United States.

It didn't take her too long before she found a real estate site that promised to let her look at various properties. Like many such sites on the Web, it's designed to allow the visitor to choose the type of property of interest. You can specify, for example, that you are interested in a home in Denver that faces west, has a hot tub, three bathrooms, four bedrooms and sells for less than $200,000.

So my neighbour chose her options, specifying the price range, location and amenities that she is looking for. She did this by "clicking" with her computer mouse on the appropriate boxes on the screen. Nothing happened.

So she clicked the appropriate boxes again. And again nothing happened.

A few minutes later (or perhaps it was hours later; remember, like most new computer users, she thinks that she looks dumb when she can't do something), she called me, reporting that it didn't work. "It doesn't list any properties for me," she noted with a touch of frustration.

However, when I tried to do the same thing on my computer, it worked. Hmm, I think. After trying a few obvious questions, I decided the only way to resolve the problem was by popping over. So I ventured over and had a look at her screen and saw that she was doing the right things — up to a point.

You see, the Internet site she visited was designed so that she could choose the type of properties she was interested in by clicking the boxes on the screen. But she was missing an important and rather critical step: once you clicked the boxes, you were supposed to tell the computer to go off and search for those types of properties.

If you looked further down the page — out of site, mind you — there was a button labeled "submit." You are supposed to click this button to tell the computer to go off and find the appropriate properties. But the button was hidden! You couldn't see it, unless you *knew* that you were supposed to go around looking for a button to tell the computer to do something!

No wonder she sat there waiting! Her experience is typical of many who are venturing online. If you are a new user to something like the Internet or any other computer program, and the design of whatever it is you are working with doesn't make your next steps obvious, then you might find yourself sitting and waiting for something to happen. I have visions in my mind of millions of adults, all around the world, staring patiently at the computer screens in front of them, waiting for something to happen. All because of poorly designed computer software.

> **At a software engineering course for aspiring managers the participants are asked: "If your team of programmers/analysts implemented airplane control software, and you were flying one day, finding out before take-off that this plane was one of those equipped with YOUR software, how many of you would get out?"**
>
> **All except one person raised their hands. The course instructor asked the only one to have left his hand down "What would you do?"**
>
> **"Stay in my seat — if my team wrote the software for this plane, it wouldn't move, let alone take off."**
> Seen on the Internet

The more I used computers and saw the problems that people were encountering, the more I wondered what the problem was. As I began to explore the topic, I found that there were computer experts who were clearly saying that people weren't the problem; the computer and software designs were the culprits.

With these thoughts in the back of my mind, and while undertaking the research for this book, I found that I kept coming across a fellow named Donald Norman, who had written a book initially called

The Psychology of Everyday Things and later re-released as *The Design of Everyday Things*. It turns out he is with Apple Computer, undoubtedly the most brilliant computer company that has ever existed, because the entire goal of that corporation has been to try to make computing easy.

Norman is what we might call a "design specialist." An extremely deep thinker, he is involved in trying to figure out how to make "things" easier for people to use. He is the type of fellow who might look at a door and ask the question, "Why do these devices add to the stresses of life rather than reduce them?" He'll help door manufacturers figure out how to best design a door so that by looking at it, people will know whether it is a push door or a pull door. This type of design issue has become a science.

> **Just because something doesn't do what you planned it to doesn't mean it's useless.**
>
> Thomas Alva Edison

Notes Norman in the introduction to his book, "over the years I have fumbled my way through life, walking into doors, failing to figure out water faucets, incompetent at working the simple things of every day life." And like many of us, he often wondered whether he was simply a klutz, until he realized that others had the same frustrations and problems. "And we all seemed to blame ourselves," noting the tendency where we all think we are rather stupid if we don't "get it."

In his book Norman explains that the designs of many of the things we take for granted in our lives are simply poorly thought-out, with the result that we experience great frustration in trying to use many things. He describes it as the "hidden frustration of everyday things"; not just devices such as computers, but everything from doors to fax machines, photocopiers and clock radios.

Reading his work, you appreciate that maybe we aren't so stupid after all; just maybe we live in a world in which many things haven't been designed for basic "human usability."

I think all of us would agree with that line of thinking, and I am sure we can all remember any number of situations where something seemed to be too complex for its own good.

In my case, I remember back in 1989 when the company I worked for first introduced a fancy new telephone system with voice mail. It was so new — and so fancy — that everyone in the office had to take a one-hour "course" to learn how to use it. Imagine, we had to take a course to learn how to use a telephone! Looking back, I wonder if it is things like this that point to the fact that perhaps we have lost our collective sanity as a society.

> **For a list of all the ways technology has failed to improve the quality of life, please press three.**
>
> Alice Kahn

Thinking back about that one particular experience, I realized what had happened: the designers, telephone system engineers mostly, in the 1980s took the most marvelously simple invention, the telephone, and crammed it full of all kinds of new capabilities. By doing so, they made it so complex that many of us couldn't begin to fathom how to use it! In effect, they set out to destroy the simplicity of what is perhaps the easiest-to-use invention of the industrial age. After all, when you were growing up, you didn't have to learn how to use a telephone, did you? You instinctively knew simply by watching someone else that all you had to do was dial the number of the person you wished to call, and magic would happen.

> **Perhaps the most frustrating technology to us involves what many people now call "voice mail jail." You probably have experienced the type of situation outlined below, taken from an online newsletter on the Internet, in which you find it impossible to reach someone. This is a good example of what goes wrong when a lousy job is done with the design of a new technology and is indicative of a design problem.**
>
> **IF YOU KNOW THE NUMBER OF THE PERSON YOU'RE CALLING, PLEASE DIAL IT NOW. OTHERWISE WAIT ON THE LINE AND AN OPERATOR WILL ASSIST YOU.**
>
> [126]

SORRY, THERE IS NO EXTENSION 126. IF YOU KNOW THE NUMBER OF THE PERSON YOU'RE CALLING, PLEASE DIAL IT NOW. OTHERWISE WAIT ON THE LINE AND AN OPERATOR WILL ASSIST YOU.

[wait]

IF YOU KNOW THE NUMBER OF THE PERSON YOU'RE CALLING, PLEASE DIAL IT NOW. OTHERWISE WAIT ON THE LINE AND AN OPERATOR WILL ASSIST YOU.

[Hmmm. It is in a loop. What if I dial '0'?]

HI THIS IS ANN. I'M NOT IN THE OFFICE TODAY. PLEASE LEAVE A MESSAGE AT THE SOUND OF THE BEEP.

BEEP.

[Hmm. Didn't work. Hang up and dial again.]

IF YOU KNOW THE NUMBER OF THE PERSON YOU'RE CALLING, PLEASE DIAL IT NOW. OTHERWISE WAIT ON THE LINE AND AN OPERATOR WILL ASSIST YOU.

[wait]

ONE MOMENT PLEASE, YOUR CALL IS BEING TRANSFERRED TO AN OPERATOR.

HI THIS IS ANN. I'M NOT IN THE OFFICE TODAY. PLEASE LEAVE A MESSAGE AT THE SOUND OF THE BEEP.

BEEP.

[Sigh, hang up]

Today? That simplicity is being ruined through voice mail, conference call capabilities, speed dial, busy-dial return functions and all kinds of other "modern" features. The result? Companies send staff on "courses" where they are supposed to learn how to use a telephone! After taking the course, staff come back to their offices and marvelous new office telephones, crammed full of all kinds of special buttons and features that let them do all kinds of special things. And most of them go merrily along punching in the phone number of the person they wish to call and ignore all the other special features.

Study after study has shown that most people use very few, if any, of the special features of their telephone. It has been overdesigned and made too complex. And as for voice mail, I applaud the decision of a massive worldwide computer company to abandon it!

> **Computer technology is still young, still exploring its potential. The notion lingers that if you have not passed the secret rites of initiation into programming skills, you should not be allowed into the society of computer users. It is like the early days of the automobile: only the brave, the adventurous, and the mechanically sophisticated need apply.**
> Donald A. Norman, *The Design of Everyday Things* (Bantam Doubleday Dell Publishing, New York, 1988)

Have things gone too far? Don Norman thinks so. In his book he holds forth a special disdain for the design of computer technology; it's "an area where all the major difficulties of design can be found in profusion."

He clearly lays the blame on the fact that most of the ways in which we interact with computers have been dictated by computer programmers and engineers. "Designers of computer systems seem particularly oblivious to the needs of users, particularly susceptible to the pitfalls of design. The professional design community is seldom called in to help with computer products. Instead, design is left in the hands of engineers and programmers, people who usually have no experience, and no expertise in designing for people."

Re-read that last phrase: *they have no expertise in designing for people.* As Norman puts it, "that is not their expertise, nor should it be."

Consider this: here you are, stressed about your complex relationship with computer technology. Day by day you struggle to deal with the computer revolution that surrounds you, convinced that you are the problem. And now you read that one of the world's leading researchers into how to make things easier to use states that the problem isn't you. The problem is the fact that much of the stuff you might use on a computer is designed by people who have absolutely no concept of how to make it easy to use! Are you starting to feel better? You should.

The problems of computer design have come to be recognized through the last decade because of folks like Don Norman. People listen to him when he talks about the problems posed by lousy design and increasing complexity. It's his belief that the more features that are added to something, the more difficult it becomes to use. He thinks that if you double the number of features on something, you quadruple the complexity. Triple the number of features, and the complexity grows ninefold. Add four times the features, and you get 16 times the complexity.

> **Most programmers are ill-equipped to figure out how office workers and other nontechnical users best handle computers. So companies are bringing in professionals from disciplines as far afield as education and psychology to help in the design of man-to-machine communications. AT & T, for example had a staff of psychologists survey about 400 computer users to help it decide how to add commands to its Unix operating system.**
> "Software: the New Driving Force," *Business Week*, February 27, 1984, in *The Information Technology Revolution*, edited by T. Forester (MIT Press, Cambridge, Massachusetts, 1985)

> **Relative calm is expected in South Central Los Angeles for the next several weeks, as looters stay home and try to program their new VCR's.**
> Weekend news report, seen on the Internet

The reality is that we live in a world of ever-increasing complexity; many of us cannot fathom the wildly complex devices in our lives, simply because many of them have not been designed to make it easy for us to understand them! Why should we possibly feel stupid? We should feel absolutely brilliant for having come this far!

A few years back *Business Week* ran an article that noted an increasing trend for simpler and more straightforward design. People like Don Norman were making their presence felt.

> In 1962 at Lincoln Labs...Ivan Sutherland demonstrated a program called Sketchpad...Sutherland sat in front of a screen and, using a light pen, drew engineering drawings.... Sutherland had invented the field of computer graphics 20 years early.
>
> To Alan Kay, a talented young computer scientist who would become a prime mover in personal computing, Sutherland's achievement was stunning: "You can't buy a system today that does all the things that Sketchpad could back then. That's what's really amazing. It had the first system that had a window, first system that had icons, certainly the first system to do all of its interactions through the display itself. And for a small number of people in this community, the Advance Research Projects Agency research community, this system was like seeing a glimpse of heaven. Because it had all of the kinds of things that the computer seemed to promise...you could...think of it...as a light that was sort of showing us the way."
>
> Jon Palfreman and Doron Swade, The Dream Machine — Exploring the Computer Age (BBC Books, London, 1991)

Today, take a look at the number of options on your remote control and ask yourself if you actually use all those buttons, and then take a look at some of the new ones being sold in stores today. You'll find an effort towards simplicity, because worldwide, the electronics business has been doing what it can to reduce the complexity of such devices.

When it comes to computer software, a similar trend has been underway based on research that actually began in 1962 and given credence with the arrival of the Apple Macintosh, what is arguably still the friendliest and easiest-to-use computer on the planet. The brilliance of Apple was that it quickly came to recognize that it wasn't people who needed fixing; it was the computer and the "interface," or method, by which people interact with computers. Apple went so far as to hire Don Norman to help them deal with the problem.

Elsewhere in the computer industry, a field of study that has existed for some time has finally come to be recognized: HCI, or human-computer interaction. Today, psychologists, design experts, artists, engineers and programmers are all getting involved in trying to improve the way the computer works, to make it easier for normal folks to comprehend what to do.

An entire profession is being launched on the foundation of the admission that most computer programs and software to this point have been nothing less than completely dreadful. Understanding this should provide us some pretty powerful enthusiasm to march ahead, rather than holding ourselves back. As you deal with the subject of computers, always remember these fundamentals:

1. You shouldn't feel bad if you don't "get it"; after all, the computer industry has finally admitted that these things have not been easy to use.

2. Technology is complex, and if we don't have the natural inclination to easily understand it, comprehend it or figure it out, we will be challenged by it. This is a natural state of being for many people.

3. Things will continue to become easier to learn, but until they do, they will be difficult!

4. Take credit for your accomplishments so far; everything that you have managed to do with your computer is a step in the right direction and an indication that you are on the right track!

5. When befuddled by your computer, look around for the thing that isn't obvious. It's probably the thing that will work.

10

Shopping in a State of Confusion

Everything is easy as long as you are not the schmuck who has to implement it.

Seen on the Internet

While writing this book, I undertook to help out my brother-in-law. After all, I had finally convinced him that if he bought just a little bit more memory for his computer, it would make a big difference in the speed of the machine. He finally agreed, as long as I went out to buy it, since he didn't have a clue what to ask for.

No problem for me! I have lots of computer bravado; I dabble with everything involving my computers, and I like to think that I'm on top of the situation. You could say I'm a bit of a dweeb, since I'm regularly adding new equipment to my own PC. Heck, I've gone so far as to install hard drives and tape drives and memory on my own. However, just to be safe, I obtained the manual for the computer from my brother-in-law before I ventured out.

One day, actually, two days before Christmas, I trotted off to a computer store, my family in tow, confident of what I was doing. I chose a store at random; for this type of thing, virtually any computer store will do, large or small.

I went up to the counter. Five metres away, three fellows sat, talking with each other, oblivious to my entrance. They were debating something or other about some piece of software. Pretending to ignore them, I looked at some computer things in a display case, figuring that one of them would soon come over to me with the obligatory welcome message, "Can I help you?"

> Many of us feel intimidated when confronted with the inevitability of starting over with a new computer or upgrading the old one. It's a bit like dealing with mechanics or autobody companies if you live where salt is the most common material between you and the asphalt. They smile and say, "Oh, we have actually had customers who had gone a full year without seeing new rust." With computers, just read "A full year without being embarrassingly obsolete."
>
> "Taking The FUD* Out of Buying a Computer," *The Computer Paper*, January, 1996

Two minutes later, they were still debating. "Excuse me," I said, wondering if these guys knew anything about customer service. One of them came over, at which point we began a five-minute exploration into my purchase plans. Now remember, I thought I knew what I needed.

But this fellow started peppering me with questions, some of which I couldn't answer. "Does it take 60 nanosecond or 70 nanosecond RAM," he asked. "Does it need pairs, or can it take singles? Are you sure you can only add one?" Uncertainty began to build. "Is it EDO or not? That makes a difference," he said.

On and on he went, finally getting to my final question, no, I wouldn't be able to return it if it didn't work. I left quickly. I slunk out of the store, my head down in shame. Like many people venturing into a computer store, I had failed in my quest.

> **The teacher pretended that algebra was a perfectly natural affair, to be taken for granted, whereas I didn't even know what numbers were. Mathematics classes became sheer terror and torture to me. I was so intimidated by my incomprehension that I did not dare to ask any questions.**
> Carl Jung

Driving home, I began to think about my experience. Certainly the demeanour of the salesman was less than helpful. In fact, in retrospect, it was almost contemptuous, in that I did not know enough about what I needed to buy. How dare I come into his store so ill-prepared! Wait a moment, I thought! I was intimidated by this guy! And if I'm a bit of a dweeb and know what I'm doing, and I can be intimidated, what about everyone else? My intimidation turned to anger.

The entire process of buying a computer has proven to be one of the most intimidating, confusing and challenging exercises of this century. If you have been through the experience, you know what I mean. And if you came out of it feeling like a real dummy and thinking that you must be the only person in the world who didn't have a good idea of what you were doing, don't!

Simply, it's not something that is easy to do. This is evidenced by the fact that there has been and is still a wealth of information devoted to trying to help people figure out how to buy a computer! Television shows and radio programs have examined the topic. Community colleges, high schools, adult education programs and other institutions have put together seminars — even courses several weeks long — that examine the issue in-depth.

In addition to all this, the computer industry devotes a lot of time and resources trying to ease their existing and potential customers into the minefield of computer technology. They distribute brochures, provide marketing seminars, offer the support of their help desks and expend a lot of time and energy trying to help the customer understand just what it is he or she should want to buy.

And it's such a complex area that entire books have been written about the topic; in Canada, a book titled *How to Buy a Computer*, by Myles White, has sold some 18,000 copies.

Even the Massachusetts Institute of Technology has gone so far as to run a series of seminars for their students and the general public entitled "Everything You Always Wanted to Know about Buying a Computer (But Were Afraid to Ask)." One of the world's leading hi-tech institutions needs to run a course to help people understand how to buy something? That in itself is indicative that you are not alone.

I've always wondered about this peculiar state of affairs. Have you ever seen a newspaper article on "how to buy a toaster oven"? Or a television show called "Important Things to Consider Before Buying a Fridge"? How about a book, "101 Questions to Ask Before Committing to a New Sofa"? Of course not! And that's precisely why so many people come away feeling bruised by the experience.

> **What we call progress is the exchange of one nuisance for another nuisance.**
>
> Henry Havelock Ellis

The reality is that if you haven't taken the time to learn all about computers, and if you haven't mastered terms like Pentium, sound cards, audio cards, memory, RAM, hard drives, CD-ROMs and everything else, you won't be quite sure what exactly you should be looking for. You'll venture into a computer store and will soon find yourself dealing with the arrogance of a salesperson, usually a kid or someone in his 20s, who has mastered all of those terms. They can run roughshod over you and your ignorance, and often do.

What happens to thousands of people every day? They come away from the experience of purchasing a computer — or upgrading an existing one — with any number of emotions. They're frustrated, confused, intimidated, angry and more than likely concerned that they might not have bought the right thing. Some feel ripped off. Then finally, they get it home, attempt to set it up, and try to get everything working. That, too, is an experience.

> **No matter how many times you've bought a computer, the process is fraught with hazards. Like making sure you get the right system for your needs, one that won't be out of date before you plug it in, one that actually works like it's supposed to. Even experienced buyers can get taken advantage of — and if you've never bought a computer before, you may feel defeated before you even begin.**
>
> **The trick is to stay in charge of the process.**
>
> Seen on the Internet

A few days after my neighbours bought their new home PC, they gave me a call; they had a problem with their printer. Nothing unusual; it had suddenly stopped working, and they didn't have a clue what to do to solve the problem.

I wandered over and had a look to see what was wrong. It turned out to be a tiny piece of paper jammed in the printer, causing the printer to think that it was out of paper. This, of course, meant that it refused to print anything else. Since they hadn't spent much time in their lives battling with printers, they wouldn't have known exactly what to look for. As for myself, I'm a regular contender in the ring against the machines, so I had an inkling of what might be wrong.

While there, I spent a few minutes inspecting their new computer. It was a fine machine, from one of the world's leading computer manufacturers. But what immediately struck me was the sheer amount of stuff that came with it. All kinds of disks, boxes, manuals, brochures. They hadn't bought a computer; they had bought a warehouse! Or so it seemed. Much of this stuff came for free with the computer and was already installed; you see, these days computer manufacturers are providing all kinds of free stuff to entice the purchaser into thinking that their computer is better than the other guy's.

Of course, the immediate challenge for them was merely to comprehend what they had just bought. The result, of course, when I visited them, was a jumble of manuals all over the table, and a computer screen that looked like the battle of Normandy was about to take place, as different software vied for their attention. It was as if they had bought a car that had hundreds of gadgets, most of which they would never use, and all they wanted was a car that would get them to the grocery store for some milk. You wouldn't believe what came preinstalled on their machine! I was so intrigued I took an inventory.

There were five programs to help them explore the online world, three different programs for sending and receiving faxes, a home gardening program, an encyclopedia on CD-ROM, something called the "Widget Workshop" (I still haven't figured out what this one does), various computer and mouse control programs, a "diagnostic" program, a security program and programs to do a backup and check for "viruses."

There were several programs for young children, plus Photoworks, Quicken and TurboTax, the Rand McNally Tripmaker and various programs from Microsoft. There's more, but I won't bother listing the rest.

"Do you know what you have on this machine?" I asked them. No, they answered.

"Did you try any of it out?" Not really; they've tried a few of the things, but weren't quite sure of everything that they had or what it could be used for.

> **The last time somebody said, "I find I can write much better with a word processor," I replied, "They used to say the same thing about drugs."**
> Roy Blount, Jr.

"Would you know how to get rid of it if you had to?" No.

So here we have it: across Canada and around the world, millions of people are buying computers, many of which come preloaded with all kinds of stuff, much of which most people don't use because they aren't quite sure what they have.

> **Documentation is like sex; when it's good, it's very, very good, and when it's bad, it's better than nothing.**
> Seen on the Internet

I've learned a lot from my neighbours about the state of computers in the world. Along with all the software that came with their new computer was plenty of documentation. For me, the documentation that comes with computer hardware and software is nothing less than a source of wonder and awe.

After all, where else could you find a statement like "you can print a worksheet showing the worksheet frame, grid lines, charts and other drawn objects; or you can hide these elements for print. For example, for your own reference, one printed version of a worksheet could show grid lines and the worksheet frame and hide drawn objects. Another version, for presentation, could hide the frame and grid lines, but show all the charts and other drawn objects." Uh-huh.

Documentation for computer hardware is perhaps even more fascinating than that for software. Open a manual, and you can encounter any number of gems. Such as, "the parallel port category configures the system's built-in parallel port. This category can be set to 378H, 278H or 3BCH to automatically configure the port, or it can be set to OFF to disable the port." OK, sure.

At some point while using a computer program, you'll click on the button labeled "help." But that's not always what you will get. My wife uses a popular program to prepare information for distribution on my World Wide Web site on the Internet. It's a program that is often promoted to the general public as being "user-friendly," a straightforward tool that anyone could learn to use.

Since she needed some help on how to do something at one point, she pressed the help key. This is part of the explanation that she got:

> When the ACTION attribute is set to an HTPP URL, the METHOD attribute must be set to an HTTP method as defined by the HTTP method specification in the IETF draft HTTP standard. The default METHOD is GET, although for many applications, the POST method may be preferred. With the post method, the ENCTYPE attribute is a MIME type specifying the format of the posted data; by default, is application/x-www-form-urlencoded.

Is it any wonder many people in our generation are intimidated by the wired world, when this is the "help" we get?

Why is this so? Often, because the documentation and help screens are sometmes written by people least capable of doing so, programmers. As noted by Albert Mehrabian, Ph.D., Professor of Psychology, "the logic and organization of software manuals are often dictated by programmers who have worked for lengthy periods on various features of the software. Such persons are far too close to the product to be able to perceive it from the perspective of the end user. As a consequence, most manuals are communication disasters!"

> **Common problems shared by manuals is that they show a lack of understanding of user needs and, instead, are written to show off the complexity and versatility of a product...Readers must wade through massive amounts of confusing material even to learn about some of the most essential and elementary features of the software (e.g., sometimes, even something as basic as how to start a program or how to quit).**
>
> Albert Mehrabian, Ph.D., Professor of Psychology, UCLA

I raise these points as a way of providing you some encouragement. You aren't alone in your confusion and frustration; many people who have bought a computer or upgraded their existing ones have gone through a lot of bad experiences.

> **One of the greatest discoveries a man makes, one of his great surprises, is to find he can do what he was afraid he couldn't do.**
>
> Henry Ford

Whether plunging in for the first time, or if you've been doing this for years, it can only help you to recognize that in some ways, the odds are stacked against you. It's a battle — you against them — and you have to come out on top. I have a few suggestions:

1. When you meet someone and he is talking in technical terms, interrupt him and ask for human terms! Refuse intimidation! Fight back! Ask for explanations in terms *you* can understand!

2. If someone is too technical, call his bluff; you might even discover that he doesn't really know what he is talking about, since he doesn't really understand it either. He may be using fancy words and phrases just to try to impress you. As Peter Legge notes in his book, *How to Soar with The Eagles* (Eaglet Publishing, Burnaby, B.C., 1992), "I've been told that we may feel like fools for five minutes by asking the wrong question. But by never asking a question, we will remain fools forever."

3. If the technology frightens you, work to overcome it! Pace yourself; try to learn one new thing related to your system every day, and start with the simple stuff, like understanding what each part of your computer can do or learning some of the jargon. Nobody says you have to be a technical genius or that you should turn into the ultimate computer geek. But you need to have some knowledge of what is going on in order to master it.

4. Don't hesitate to sit down with a friend/colleague and ask for some help. Do the same for others, too! You can learn a lot when you have to try to teach or explain it to someone else.

5. If you have a child who is good with technology, change places with her. Let her be the teacher and you the pupil!

6. Instead of trying to figure something out from the manual, figure it out from doing. Press a few buttons, try what might be logical and learn by intuition and logic.

7. Do some reading. Search out those computer magazines and columns specializing in reaching normal folks like yourself; avoid the highly technical ones. Take your time in reading them, and think about what is being said. Before you know it, the articles will have a familiar ring to them, and you will start to see that it really is not that overwhelming if you take it one step at a time.

And don't feel bad if you've had a bad experience buying or upgrading a PC! Refuse to accept the intimidation of the information age and those who command it, and you'll come out ahead.

11

The Futz Factor

Variations on Murphy's Law, specifically for computers:
Everything takes longer than you think.
And experience is what causes a person to make
new mistakes instead of old ones.

Seen on the Internet

There is another variation on Murphy's Law that seems very specific to the experiences that most people have with computers: anything that begins badly, ends badly. Of course, some people have a more extreme perspective: anything that begins badly, ends worse.

Clearly, the computer industry presents a message that is often complex and incomprehensible to the neophyte user; we've seen that with software, documentation, manuals and with the attitude of the computer industry. But it's not just the computer novice who is confused and frustrated; even skilled veterans can find the whole darn thing to be a challenge. One reason has to do with what I call the "futz factor."

> **"Westheimer's Rule": to estimate the time it takes to do a task: estimate the time you think it should take, multiply by two and change the unit of measure to the next highest unit. Thus, we allocate two days for a one hour task.**
>
> Seen on the Internet

What's that, you say? We futz away time with our computers; "futzing" is the tendency where people end up wasting a lot of time learning about computers, waiting for them to do something, and solving the little, mundane problems that occur day-to-day as they struggle to master their machines. Surely as a novice or expert computer user, you've experienced the futz factor:

- You try to print something, and it doesn't print. Once you figure out what you think the problem is, you manage to get it to print. Except it doesn't print exactly what you wanted, so you try again. This time, it prints the whole thing, but it's obvious that something is out of whack: there are funny characters all over the page! You try to figure out what has gone wrong.

- You've spent a lot of time learning a particular computer program and finally get things working just fine. Then you rush out to get the new, "upgraded" version, tempted by all the new features that are promised in the marketing literature and in the computer press. Once you figure out how to install the new version, which sometimes takes the better part of a day, you find that you suddenly can't read your old information files. You end up frittering away even more time trying to solve that problem, only to discover days later that the manual that came with the upgrade forgot to tell you about an important step you were supposed to do.

- You start to use the new version of the program and discover that nothing works like it used to; there are new buttons, new commands and new ways of doing things. You end up spending hours and hours trying to figure out how to do simple things once again.

- Once you install the new program, you often discover that it either causes other programs to stop working or everything on your computer fails altogether!

Of course, I haven't mentioned what happens when you install new hardware on your computer. Whether you upgrade the memory, add a CD-ROM, buy a new printer or do anything else that involves a physical device, something is bound to go wrong. The futz factor kicks in!

I have experienced the "futz factor" many times. One of the most memorable occurrences happened on a cold January evening a few years ago. It was late, past 10:00 p.m., and I was struggling to put the final touches on a book that I had co-authored. I expected to spend five or ten minutes making a few changes to some diagrams, after which I would transmit the finished book to my publisher. On deadline and on time.

This was one of my first books; it was related to the Internet. The book featured various diagrams and charts in several chapters. To handle those with ease, I had purchased — for $129 — the latest upgrade to the word processing software that I used to write the book. The reason? The new version had the dandy feature that it could automatically obtain information from other programs, so I could easily deal with and manage all the different charts and graphs that I had prepared for the book. I figured that using the new version would make it easier for me to pull the book together. And it had, so far.

> **Another variation on Murphy's Law that seems to be computer-specific: Not until a program has been in production for six months will the most harmful error be discovered.**
>
> Seen on the Internet

It was all fairly sophisticated stuff, the way it was supposed to work. But that night, when I went to make one final change to a diagram...

Wham! My computer froze. Nothing worked — not the mouse, not the keyboard. The only thing I could do was kill the power to the machine, which, of course, meant that I lost all the changes that I had made since I last saved stuff an hour ago! The "futz factor" had taken hold.

By 2:30 a.m., I had figured out what went wrong and was trying to fix the diagram, since it had now become a bunch of meaningless garbage.

At 3:00 a.m., I discovered that the problem had trashed some other diagrams in that chapter. And so began a lengthy battle that lasted until 10:00 a.m. such that some 12 hours after I began, I finally started to transmit the chapters to my publisher.

Struggling to stay awake, I had to wonder whether computer technology and the visions promoted by the computer industry that it is all so easy are simply beyond the truth. The computer industry doesn't like to talk about the futz factor. It's no wonder.

You should understand the way the software industry works. It has, for example, a distinctly different concept of the words "quality control" and enjoys releasing new versions of stuff on a regular basis. It is said that any particular software program will undergo a number of releases in the first several years. Each release is given a number by the software company called the version number — I suspect, so that they know which bugs exist in which version when you call them with a problem.

> **Computers make it easier to do a lot of things, but most of the things they make it easier to do don't need to be done.**
> Andy Rooney

The program is first released as version 1.0 and is sometimes released as a "beta version," with a number less than 1.0. Whatever the case, this means that the program is brand new, full of bugs and simply doesn't work right. In effect, as soon as you buy the product, you've unknowingly been recruited as a quality control tester for the company, without remuneration.

So immediately upon using the program, you will find bugs and you will encounter untold frustration. After all, it's been rushed to market in order to raise the company some much-needed money: they need it to hire staff to fix the bugs!

Regardless of the fact that it is new and unproven, version 1.0 might be used by millions of people for a few weeks, months or years, all of whom will invariably discover that they spend a lot of time futzing with it to try to get it to work right or to get around the problems that it presents.

Soon, a version 1.1 is rushed to market; it fixes the worst bugs that people reported in version 1.0. At this time, a great deal of marketing hype is generated by the company, letting people know that the worst of the problems have been solved.

The reality? Plenty of bugs remain; they just hide for a little while until the company has shipped thousands of copies of the new version, at which point they show themselves by crashing computers across the country.

Of course, this means that months later, the developer releases a version 1.2 that solves some of the other problems that had been reported in version 1.1. But this time, there are no press releases, marketing announcements or other information; the company doesn't want to let people know that there were more problems than they admitted to!

At some point between version 1.1 and 1.2, the company decides that a "rewrite" is necessary, based on the customer and industry feedback they have been receiving. They undertake a massive change to the program, adding all kinds of new features, often changing it to such an extent that it looks completely different. It's such a significant change that the version is awarded the number 2.0. They release it at a new price that is twice as high as the old one.

The new software is released to much fanfare. It's "revolutionary," "state-of-the-art" and "amazing"! Hype rules! The marketing department has gone into overdrive to make the world aware that the release of the new software is perhaps one of the most significant developments in the history of mankind.

Unfortunately, they fell victim to "second-system effect" and added so much new stuff to the program that what once shipped on 2 diskettes now ships on 37 diskettes and a CD-ROM! You buy it and discover that you probably need to buy a new computer or upgrade your existing one in order to have any hope of using it! Not to mention the fact that it has ten times more bugs than the original version 1.0 had!

> **All technology should be assumed guilty until proven innocent.**
>
> David Brower

> **Definition:**
> **Second-system effect: n (sometimes, more euphoniously, "second-system syndrome"). When one is designing the successor to a relatively small, elegant, and successful system, there is a tendency to become grandiose in one's success and design an elephantine feature-laden monstrosity.**
> Found in the "Jargon File" on the Internet

As soon as you get your version 2.0 working, you find out that version 2.1 has been released, once again, very quietly, to fix some of the bugs that existed in version 2.0, including those that have caused you problems. You upgrade to 2.1, only to find that you can't read your old data anymore.... The cycle goes on...and on...and on.

And by the way, in most cases, you have to pay for the upgrade that will fix your problems. The industry seems to think that we should consider ourselves privileged to be using their software, bugs or no bugs.

Reality? The software industry makes billions of dollars, and we futz away our time with their software. If the automobile industry released cars the way the software industry released programs, we'd be driving buckets of bolts, held together by string and wax.

The futz factor doesn't involve just software; it can take over your relationship with a particular piece of hardware. In my case, I've had an ongoing battle with printers for several years. For a while, it got to the point that my wife would run from the room when I used the printer. She knew that as soon as I tried to print something, it wouldn't work and that I would get frustrated to the point that I would either yell at the machine, curse my computer or give up and ask her to do it. The latter would always solve the problem.

> **Never fight with an inanimate object.**
> P.J. O'Rourke

For some strange reason, I just couldn't get the printer to co-operate with me. I don't know exactly what it was, other than the futz factor. Any software program that I used — no matter what I did — caused a printing problem.

Then mysteriously, one day, my problems with printers went away, after one day, when I decided to hook the printer up to my wife's computer instead. I could now access the printer through the network that we have. And so today, I can finally live with my printer in peaceful coexistence; I guess it has decided to accept me as I am.

My wife, however, can't seem to get along with it anymore. I now run from the office every time she uses it, since I know that she will yell at the machine, curse her computer or give up and ask me to do it. I dread the day we have to buy a new printer, since I fear that we will never be able to print again.

> **American companies spent $1 trillion on fancy computer systems in the last decade with almost no gain in productivity.**
> "Consider the PC Paradox," *Newsweek*, February 27, 1995

Several years ago, the business press was agog with reporting about the "productivity paradox." It had discovered that corporate America had spent trillions of dollars on technology and was searching for the

> **The goal of all inanimate objects if to resist man and ultimately defeat him.**
>
> Russell Baker

missing productivity gains. The answer to me is easy: it's the futz factor. I remember reading one article around that time that the average employee spends up to 50 minutes a week learning about PCs and setting up software and trying to get everything working right. That's a lot of wasted time.

Then I came across another report which indicated that most staff in companies end up spending *5.1 hours each week* — five times the effort in the previous report — "futzing" with their computers. Some estimates have said that North American business is futzing away about 5 billion hours a year at a cost of $100 billion.

> **The services sector spent over $750 billion on information technology hardware in the 1980s and US$862 billion in the past 10 years (representing about 85% of total U.S. IT hardware investments). The service industry's investment in information technology in the 1980s was accompanied by an average productivity growth of 0.7 percent, a rate significantly lower than in the 1970s and much below that of the manufacturing sector during the decade of the eighties.**
>
> Blake Ives, Editor's Comments, in *Management Information System Quarterly*, Vol. 18, No. 2, June, 1994

The news reports at the time were staggering in their shock and outrage; headlines screamed that literally trillions and trillions of dollars were being spent on information technology for which there was no return. Respected publications such as *Business Week*, *Forbes* and the *Harvard Business Review* undertook lengthy essays and analyses to understand what was going wrong, seeking complicated answers for a simple problem. Couldn't they see that it's the futz factor!

Thus it has been proven that there is a real and significant problem in the computer industry. Few of the companies that develop the stuff that we use day-to-day have caught onto the concept of KISS: Keep It Simple, Stupid.

Through the last several years, I've come to realize one of the main culprits leading to the futz factor is the fact that the computer programs that we are using are becoming far too powerful and sophisticated for what we want to do. There is a massive gap between the power of the machines and our ability to master that power. We should not feel in the least bit bad that we find it difficult to close the gap.

Obviously, sophisticated technology presents anyone with an opportunity for productivity improvements and the opportunity to enhance our capabilities. Yet at the same time it presents the chance for a lot of wasted time — futzing.

> It's a funny thing about life; if you refuse to accept anything but the best, you very often get it.
>
> W. Somerset Maugham

What does all of this tell you? Several things should guide you in the way that you adopt and use technology:

1. Don't think that you have to use the new version, every time! Every time you get something new for your computer, you'll end up futzing away time. In many cases, you won't need the features found in the new version. Avoid marketing hype, and be judicious in your decision to go with new stuff, by recognizing that perhaps it will do you more harm than good.

2. Recognize that there are those who need to upgrade. Getting new computer software is a fix for a software junkie; there are people who thrive on this stuff. It doesn't have to be you! If you want to resist the pressure to keep moving forward with the industry at a furious pace, do so!

3. Don't feel like you are left behind! The hype generated by the industry is specifically done with the intent of making you feel that if you aren't completely up-to-date in what you use, then

you are not with it. Don't fall for it; always use the rule that if you can do what you need to do, then things must be OK.

4. Tape Murphy's Law above your computer, and always have a look at it when things go wrong! Because things will, over and over again! It's the nature of the futz factor.

5. Recognize that you are not alone; there are thousands of other people like you who encounter the futz factor on a day-to-day basis!

12

A Day in the Life of the Help Desk

> *A strong technical background was an absolute necessity for computer ownership, because most microcomputers in early 1977 were sold in kit form and required thousands of solder connections and dozens of tests to assemble. Getting a computer to work was a formidable challenge; doing anything useful with it sometimes seemed impossible.*
>
> Things the Manual Never Told You, IBM PC edition, compiled by the Boston Computer Society, edited by Jack McGrath
> (Addison-Wesley Longman Inc., Boston, 1985)

By this point, I've probably managed to convince you that a lot of the challenges that you might encounter with technology aren't necessarily your fault; you've had some pretty big hurdles to overcome, with arrogant computer people, lousy software and manuals written in some type of language clearly not intended for the common computer user. Even so, you likely remain frustrated on a day-to-day basis.

That's OK. Recognize that even as you struggle along and master some aspects of this new world of technology, there continue to be all kinds of other people who face continual challenges, no matter how hard they try. It's OK to make mistakes; you only really fail if you don't bother to try new things at all!

You might be motivated to continue with your struggles with technology, or might gain more of a willingness to try something new, if you can laugh at yourself and with others. Humour, after all, is sometimes the best weapon in dealing with adversity.

A good starting point for such humour is to appreciate what the folks who work at customer support help desks go through, for they are the people who encounter the true magic of this strange, evolving relationship that we have with technology.

> A tech support guy once told me that he got a call from someone saying that the computer screen just went black and the computer wouldn't respond at all. The tech guy (starting with the obvious) asked the guy if the computer was still plugged in and that maybe his foot had knocked the plug out of the socket. The guy on the other end of the phone said to hold on — that he would be back in a minute with a flashlight because the electricity had just gone out in his building and he couldn't see under the desk without the lights....
>
> Seen on the Internet

Keep this fact in mind: the high-profile heroes of the computer revolution are *not* guys like Bill Gates of Microsoft, an individual who makes so much money that when the stock market has a good day, he earns a couple of hundred million dollars.

The real unsung heroes of the computer revolution work away in silent obscurity, doing some of the most frustrating work in the industry. They provide their services to the common citizen, from within customer support departments of computer and telecommunication companies and within all kinds of corporations and organizations. They work in departments such as the "help desk," the "customer support desk" and "help center"; and they carry job titles to match. Their mission in life? To solve the problems that people have with new technology — computers and the programs that run on them.

During a typical day, they are called upon to deal with a myriad of problems, ranging from computers that won't start to software that won't work. Expected to be intimately familiar with all the details of the computers and programs for which they are responsible, they are required to deal with all of their callers in a professional, courteous and responsible manner.

You might have talked with them at one point. After all, if you buy a new computer or software program today, you'll usually find inside the package a folder or brochure describing how to get help. You'll see several options for how you can reach these people: a 1-800 number, an e-mail address or a Web site on the Internet. If you work in a company, your phone directory will often list the contact number for the help desk in the computer department.

And one day, you encounter a problem, so you contact them.

After a rather lengthy wait on hold, you finally get through to someone and begin to describe your problem. You hope for success. You've reached the experts. Actually, it's more likely that you are talking to a kid fresh out of school, someone who is thrilled to have just landed his first job. Paid a mere pittance of a salary and constantly aspiring to move beyond the help desk into a real career, they find themselves on the receiving end of the frustration of the entire baby boom generation, as it struggles with new and unfamiliar technology.

Everything is funny as long as it is happening to someone else.

Will Rogers

They have a lot of stories, which we can use as a source of humour in order to better appreciate our own frailties.

> **A salesperson hoping to demonstrate to a skeptical user how easy it is to use windows:**
>
> **"Just point and click" he says. "Just point to the application you want and click on the mouse button."**
>
> **So the executive takes the mouse, lifts it, hefts it like a TV remote, points at the screen and clicks the button.**
>
> Seen on the Internet

It seems that the history of computing technology has shown that when confronted with something new and unfamiliar for the first time, many people simply don't know what to do. Since the manual is unintelligible, they try their best by marching ahead on their own. The results are often amazing.

It seems that computer disks have proven to cause the greatest confusion among new computer users and, in retrospect, are the source of much hilarity for those of us who have had similar misconceptions.

Starting in about 1985, the computer industry began to standardize the now familiar 3½-inch disks, the ones encased in hard plastic. Prior to that, most disks were 5¼-inch, with the actual disk stored inside a soft paper jacket.

The transitional period 1985 to about 1987 caused some particular challenges, as some companies discovered that people actually took scissors to their old 5¼-inch disks to try to get them to fit into the new 3½-inch disk drives, of course, not thinking that this was first of all impossible and secondly would result in the loss of substantial information on the disk even if it were possible!

> **The software inside the computer can be equally perplexing; a Dell customer called to say he couldn't fax anything. After 40 minutes of trouble shooting, the technician discovered the man was trying to fax a piece of paper by holding it in front of the screen and pressing the *send* key.**
>
> Seen on the Internet

Thank heavens the industry went to the new disks in hard plastic. One fellow at a support desk reported that in the days in which the older

5¼-inch disks were used, he was once called by a secretary who was having trouble saving information to a disk. She complained that every time she tried to, she lost some information.

Since he couldn't resolve the problem by telephone, he decided to go and visit her. He soon discovered that she was certainly doing everything right to save information to the disk, up to a point. You see, once she had saved the information to the disk, she took it out of the computer, inserted it into her typewriter, scrolled it around, and typed a label onto it. Of course, this managed to cause some rather remarkable damage to the ability of the disk to keep any kind of the information just saved to it!

Even today, some people seem confused about the simple instructions they receive from their computer that involve diskettes. For instance, when presented with the message "Insert another disk to continue," that's what they try to do — but without removing the other disk! The folks at WordPerfect reported one fellow who had managed to insert four disks and was wondering why he couldn't get the fifth into the drive.

Of course, it's not always the fault of the user; their actions are sometimes driven by the fact that they are often terrified to do anything with their computer. Terror can freeze the actions of people, as found by one company that printed three simple instructions on a label that went onto a floppy disk, thinking that they had made things as straightforward as possible for a computer user.

> **It is a mistake to suppose that men succeed through success; they much oftener succeed through failures. Precept, study, advice, and example could never have taught them so well as failure has done.**
>
> Samuel Smiles

> A classic computer support story involves the secretary who is asked to make a copy of various computer disks each night. Finally, one day, the company loses some data, and the secretary is instructed to get the disk copies. She comes back with

> a massive stack of paper, each page of which features a photocopied disk. The company never did manage to recover the lost information.
>
> Seen on the Internet

The first instruction on the label of the disk was to "insert the disk in the disk drive." They started to get calls from customers who couldn't read step 2 because the disk was in the drive! The result? The company learned that they had to be very, very clear in providing instructions.

New computer technology often poses challenges when first introduced. CD-ROMS, for instance. These days, most new computers come with CD-ROMs, devices into which you insert a round disc that looks very much like a standard CD.

One fellow called the computer company to report that the coffee cup holder on his computer broke. It took some ten minutes before a stunned computer support person realized that the guy was talking about his CD-ROM drive.

Support desks have also reported that people have complained that their CD-ROM drives aren't working when:

• they have forgotten to push the CD-ROM drawer back into the computer after putting in the disc;

• they have tried to put a regular floppy disk into the CD-ROM drive;

and

• they have forgotten to actually put the disc in the drive. They've misplaced it under some paper on their desk.

Much of the difficulty that can occur comes from the fact that new computer users are often not familiar with the special nuances or significance that certain words have in the computer industry. Microsoft Windows is a good example:

• One fellow working at a computer support desk asked the caller if he was running his program under Windows, referring to Microsoft Windows, of course. He responded, "No, my desk is next to the door."

• Another one responded, when asked if she had Windows, "No, we have air conditioning."

A computer program such as Microsoft Windows allows you to use more than one program at a time, and the terminology that is used is that each thing you might be doing runs within its own "window."

Quite often, if you have a problem and call a support desk, you'll be asked to close one or more of the windows that you have running, since that might solve the problem.

On more than one occasion, computer support staff have told the story that upon asking a caller to do that, they have heard the person get up, and the next thing they hear is the person closing windows in the room.

Computer mice pose special problems as well:

> **Would you like me to give you a formula for success? It's quite simple, really. Double your rate of failure. You are thinking of failure as the enemy of success. But it isn't at all. You can be discouraged by failure — or you can learn from it. So go ahead and make mistakes. Make all you can. Because, remember that's where you will find success.**
>
> Thomas J. Watson

• There are several reports of people complaining that the computer mouse was too difficult to use with what they called its "dust cover." The support desk soon discovered that the caller never took the mouse out of the plastic bag that it came packaged in.

> "I've pushed and pushed on this foot pedal and nothing happens," the woman replied. "Foot pedal?" "Yes," the woman

> said, "this little white foot pedal with the on switch." The *Foot pedal* it turned out was the mouse.
>
> Seen on the Internet

• Move a computer mouse across your desk, and the cursor — that little flashing thing on your computer that tells you where you are currently working — moves in the same direction. One person called a computer company and complained that when he used his computer mouse, the cursor would always go the wrong way. It turns out he was holding it backwards.

There are many more stories:

• When confronted by the computer message "Press any key to continue…" many are stunned into inaction as they search desperately for the "any" key on the keyboard.

• One individual tried to delete files on a disk using white-out.

• Another, upon encountering the message "insert floppy and close door," ran to shut the door to her office.

• One chap who, when encountering a message that said "Hit a key to continue," practically destroys his keyboard.

• One support person tells the story about the enraged caller who had to be calmed down: the caller believed that the computer had insulted him. He thought the computer was telling him he was "bad" and that he was an "invalid," when he came across the messages "Bad command or file name" and "Invalid command."

> It seems that if there is a manual and a phone side by side the phone wins every time. One frustrated customer called Compaq; they had unpacked their new Contura, plugged it in and nothing had happened for 20 minutes. When asked what happened when they pressed the power switch, they asked "What power switch."
>
> Seen on the Internet

Then there are calls to the help desk by people who report their computers aren't working. It turns out that one of several reasons applies: the power is out on the entire floor; the computer is unplugged or not turned on; the brightness is turned down all the way on the monitor; or the monitor itself isn't plugged in.

We should have some sympathy for the people who work on the computer support desks of the nation. Day after day, they are on the receiving end of calls — pleas — for help. They often end up talking to the dispirited, the hopelessly confused, the lonely — people like us. On the Internet, I came across a note about "one man from New Hampshire who calls Dell every time he experiences a life crisis. He gets a technician to walk him through some contrived problem with his computer, apparently feeling uplifted by the process."

Sometimes they'll get complaints as people deal with their rage at a problem by going over their head to management. In one case, a chap called the manager of the computer support department, complaining that he had pressed the help key 20 minutes ago, but no one had shown up yet to help him out! Ask yourself this: could you do this job?

When we were doing the research for this chapter, my wife and I spent the better part of a day finding and reading many of these computer support stories. By the end of the day, we found ourselves suffering from fits of laughter at the latest funny story that we had come across. In retrospect, it wasn't a terribly productive day, but probably one that helped to deal with the stress of a looming book deadline. And it certainly helped to shape our approach to the rest of the book, for in our humour we discovered a certain degree of humility. Like all computer users, we've had our share of "silly and stupid" mistakes.

The stories in this chapter should help you to discover a few valuable lessons:

1. You should have with you a good sense of humour about all misfortunes that might strike you in your life, even your troubles and tribulations with technology.

2. When you deal with someone at a computer help desk, appreciate that person's situation and think about some of the other callers he or she may have had! Offer a few kind words instead of venting your rage; you will probably find that he or she will respond in kind.

3. When you laugh at others, don't do so out of a sense of maliciousness but rather out of a sense that you've been there too!

13

Comprehending Geekism

As a civil engineering student Konard Zuse hated having to solve tedious and difficult calculations, and would later muse: "You could say that I was too lazy to calculate so I invented the computer."

Jon Palfreman and Doron Swade, *The Dream Machine — Exploring the Computer Age* (BBC Books, London, 1991), page 32

Each fall, 120,000 people descend upon Las Vegas. Not to gamble and not to enjoy the other pleasures of this ultimate sin city. Not at all. They are there to see and hear about the latest and greatest from the computer revolution at the annual computer trade and exhibition show known as Comdex.

> **This sort of reasoning is the long-delayed revenge of people who could not go to Woodstock because they had too much trig homework.**
> Stewart A. Baker, Chief Counsel for the U.S. National Security Agency, in *Wired Magazine*, June, 1994, commenting on the firestorm within the Internet community over plans by the government to enforce monitoring laws online, and in doing so, stating his stereotyping of computer users

It's an orgy of technological delights, and for a period of one week every year, Las Vegas contains the highest number of computer specialists ever to be assembled in one place on the planet. Since these are the same people to whom you might often be turning for help in your daily exploits with technology, it would behoove you to understand them and the culture that they live within.

From my perspective, it seems that when it comes to technology, there are two types of people: those for whom the computer is simply a useful tool and those for whom it is much more. You can be a survivor in the information age without being in the second category.

Consider the first category. There are a lot of folks like yourself. People who have struggled to figure out what they can do with their computer systems, while they go on living the rest of their day-to-day lives. For them the wired world of computers is but a means to an end.

Then there are those who have a different perspective on technology and who are more passionate about their machines. Not only do they get a thrill out of learning how to use a computer, but from understanding how it works as well. They subscribe to what I call the "WOW factor," in that they always have to be on the leading edge and live for the fascination and enchantment that come from exploring and using the latest and greatest computer technology.

They know all the right buzzwords and can open up their own computer and know what's inside — and fix it. Technology doesn't make them apprehensive; it gets them excited. They live for their machines. We sometimes call them dweebs, and we're not quite sure we understand what they are all about. We use negative terminology about them, more out of mystery than antagonism.

Everybody is ignorant, only on different subjects.

Will Rogers

But they do have an image problem. After all, when you think of a computer expert, do you visualize someone who bears a resemblance to a dashing young fighter pilot? An astronaut? A Hollywood movie hero or heroine?

Likely not. The image that comes to mind is of someone who wears glasses with lenses as thick as the bottom of a pop bottle, a short haircut and pimples. Tall, skinny and with a plastic pocket protector, they speak of nothing but computer technology in their own incomprehensible language — if they speak at all. Quiet, unassuming, they have glazed eyes that come from having stared at too many computer screens — or perhaps from eating too many Twinkies. In the book *THE DEVOURING FUNGUS: Tales of the Computer Age* (W. W. Norton, New York, 1990) Karla Jennings said that "when people think of a computer professional, they don't think of Superman or even Clark Kent, but of obnoxious creatures who prattle incomprehensibly and walk as if their pants were four sizes too small." A rather strong way of putting it.

And in fact, in our frustration, we often call them names, rather derogatory names: in addition to dweebs, we call them geeks, nerds and hackers.

> Hackers are intelligent people. They've worked with computers for years, examined them inside and out. Some have created new additions to their home computers; some have even designed their own machines. Put simply, the workings of a computer hold as much interest for hackers as the workings of a '57 Chevy do for a car fanatic.
> Neal Patrick, "Hacker Ethics," in *Digital Deli*, edited by Steve Ditlea (Workman Publishing, New York, 1984)

Just like the hot-rodders of the 1950s and current auto enthusiasts, who spend hour after hour polishing and tuning their cars to a state of perfection, computer experts understand every single part in their computers and tune their technology to a fine state of computing.

They spend their time talking about the latest cool computer hardware or debating the benefits of one particular type of computer over another. They'll wear T-shirts with the names of their favourite computer and wait eagerly for the latest software release that contains all the most recent bells and whistles.

Not only do they know how to get a particular program to work, they know how it works, why it does what it does and how to get it to stop doing what you don't want it to do! As Jennings also said in her book, "the hacker finds joy in creating programs that work, mastery in conquering the machine, and escape in marathon sessions of games."

They are masters of the computer universe, ready and able to control every aspect of their technological lives. And although brilliant, they are sometimes so immersed in the complexity of the machines they command that they cannot comprehend us mere mortals. Many are social introverts, clearly not used to dealing with people.

When we seek their help and guidance, we encounter individuals who seem to operate on a different level — and often a different planet — than the rest of us.

When we ask them a question, their response is often to roll their eyes in dismay, as if to say, "how can you be so stupid." They intimidate us.

Before the arrival of personal computers, you had to be a real computer specialist to have any involvement at all with the industry. And in the early days of the personal computer revolution, the early purchasers of technology were those who had some idea of what it was all about. The people who we sometimes call geeks and dweebs ruled the industry, with the result that for a long time — from the 1960s to the mid-1980s — the computer industry catered specifically to this crowd. To a large extent, it still does to this day.

> **In the early days of computer development, specialists in the field were very much like a priesthood, speaking their own special language, and that kept ordinary people from learning about computers.**
>
> Sanford B. Weinberg and Mark Lawrence Fuerst, *Computer Phobia — How to Slay the Dragon of Computer Fear (*Banbury Books, Pennsylvania, 1984)

Consequently, we have an industry that seems intent on focusing its marketing message and support resources on people who know all about the technology. Take a look at your average computer magazine; it is most likely geared to reach out to these "power users." Every article reports breathlessly on the latest crucial and important developments in the computer industry or how to obtain more power from your computing dollar. Columnists talk about "raging battles" between different computer companies and whether the grand vision of company X is better than that of company Y. Help columns focus on very specific details of tuning a computer to maximize performance.

It's not just magazines; many books, TV shows and syndicated radio series focus their energies on the computer expert. Conferences tend towards the technology side and feature sessions that have long, incomprehensible titles.

On top of it all, acronyms and special terminology dominate all the discussion and reporting. A voyage into the world of computer technology is a trip into a place of techno-babble.

I have a confession to make: I'm a reformed geek. You see, you don't have to be born a geek to become one; it can happen to you while you are not watching.

The signs to me weren't obvious, but looking back, they should have been. I started buying *PC Magazine* every month and looked forward with anticipation to every new software release. I hung on the word of every computer executive reported in the press, as though their pronouncements on the future could bring some type of spiritual upbringing to my life.

> **I have not lost my mind — it's backed up on disk somewhere.**
>
> Unknown

The fact that the trees were blooming in springtime wasn't important to me, but getting a new computer monitor was. I got into programming. I took the database of LP records that I had created one step further, by developing a program that would allow me to search them by the genre of music, the length of the song and other factors. I actually started developing a database of recipes, intent on using this to determine what I might eat every night.

Looking back, I must have been a rather hilarious source of amusement for many people. Based in Halifax at the time, my home was about two kilometres from the office, much of the walk home being uphill. My portable computer weighed around 15 kilograms, state-of-the-art for 1983.

Every day and every night, I carried it home and back again in a large computer bag. I still think my right arm is longer than the left. Bleary eyed, I'd come into the office each morning, lacking sleep, having spent the night before exploring the depths of the computer world exploding around me. I lived for the computer.

> Why single women should want to marry a geek:
> A) They are generally available.
> B) Other women will tend not to steal them.
> C) They can fix things.
> D) Your parents will love them.
> E) They're smart.
>
> From an Internet site entitled "Why Geek Dudes Rule"

Because the "power user" dwells on the excitement of new technology, every company in the computer industry is in a continual march forward, intent on discovering the next "great thing."

> **A geek is someone who spends time being "social" on a computer....Most geeks are technically adept and have a great love of computers, but not all geeks are programming wizards. Geeks are generally social outcasts....These are people who did not go to their high school proms, and many would be offended by the suggestion that they should have even wanted to. Geeks prefer to socialize with other geeks, the self proclaimed weird.**
>
> Found on the Internet, in a site devoted to glorification of geekdom

That's why as you deal with technology, you'll always feel like you are one step behind the rest of the crowd. And you are; power users thrive on new stuff, since the old stuff can become so boring so quickly.

Have you taken a trip to the computer magazine section of your local bookstore? Not only do they focus on the technical, but they cater to performance enhancement, as if the field of computers were some type of industry using steroids. There are hundreds of publications, with headlines announcing "screaming gigaflops," "blazing fast processors" and "the greatest in OLE/Java computability"!

The fact of the matter is that there is an entire segment within the publishing industry that is devoted to keeping these folks on top of each and every new development in the industry. Publications like *PCWeek* and *MacWorld* provide a regular update on the latest important news having to do with computer hardware, software and the online world.

And Comdex itself is indicative of the mentality of the industry. Each year, companies rush about to get new product announcements ready for the show floor, with a continual battle for one company to top the announcements made by another. In fact, the industry has become known for suffering from several significant problems. "Vaporware" is the term used to describe the products that are often announced far in advance of their actual release date, in some cases, many years in advance.

Broken promises are common; companies often announce plans to develop something, then quietly shelve those plans when it becomes impossible to deliver.

Visions dominate; it seems every few months, every computer company on the planet announces a grand plan to integrate all the complexities of the computer world into one simple, easy-to-use framework. Years later, they quietly file their vision in the trash can.

Hype is the foundation of the computer industry; after all, you can only keep the power user happy through a continual and incessant trumpeting of everything that is new. The old is out, new is cool and nothing other than the latest greatest software matters.

Given the unreality of the computer industry and the fact that it often seems to be aiming its entire message at those who are masters of their technology, should you feel bad at all if you don't think that you are completely up-to-date with everything? Not at all!

Apple Computer recognized that with so much of the computer industry focused on the computer specialist, the common user was being left out. They solved this dilemma by releasing the brilliant Macintosh computer in 1984.

Specifically aiming the computer at the non-geek crowd, they still use the marketing slogan today that bears witness to their decision: "The Computer for the Rest of Us." Everything about the machine made it the ideal tool for the novice computer user, and it remains so today, even as Apple Computer struggles to survive in an industry increasingly dominated by Microsoft.

> A computer programmer is walking along one day when the programmer hears a voice say something. He looks down and there's a frog sitting there.
>
> "Kiss me and I'll turn into a beautiful princess," says the frog.
>
> The programmer picks up the frog, smiles at it and puts it in his pocket.
>
> Puzzled the frog says, "Kiss me and I'll turn into a beautiful princess and I'll stay with you for a month."
>
> The programmer stops, pulls the frog out of his pocket, smiles at it and puts it back in his pocket.

> Still puzzled the frog says, "Ok, I'll turn into a beautiful princess, stay with you for a whole month, and do anything you want."
>
> The programmer stops, pulls the frog out of his pocket, smiles at it and puts it back in his pocket.
>
> Finally, the frog says, "Wait a minute, I've offered to stay with you for a month and do anything you want and you still won't kiss me. Why not?"
>
> "Well," says the programmer, "You see, I'm a computer programmer and I don't have the time for a girl friend, but a talking frog is cool."

Seen on the Internet

It took a long time for the rest of the computer industry to catch up with Apple, if it has at all. In fact, it would seem that only through the last several years has the industry come to realize that there are a lot of people out here who don't really care about their gigaflops and megabits and SCSI interfaces. They simply want to be able to plug in a computer and have it work without pain or complication.

Slowly, inevitably, the computer world — both the computer industry and power users — are coming to recognize that a different approach is needed to deal with the common user. That's why you'll see companies like IBM and Microsoft recognize that they have a problem and begin to focus their efforts on folks like yourself.

Should you care what power users do? Should it matter to you that the computer industry caters primarily to their needs and whims?

It certainly should, for as you muddle your way through the world of technology and try to discover your own magic from the computer world, you'll have to deal with both the power users and their own attitudes:

1. When you are seeking help, whether from a computer support desk or from a friend, you might be dealing with someone who

> **As we see people, we treat them; and as we treat them, often they become.**
>
> Nietzsche

has a different perception of the machine. If you recognize that they have different needs and wants from computers, then you might understand why they often seem so frustrated with your simple questions.

They are masters of the computer universe; they get it all and often cannot comprehend why you do not. They cannot fathom why you don't understand it, leading to a communication problem that is unique in its unbreachability.

2. It also can't hurt you to realize that the computer industry itself is still learning how to deal with someone like you. For such a long time, everything it did focused on the dweeb. Along came someone like yourself — and many millions of others — and the computer industry was never quite sure how to react.

Today, I don't consider myself to be a dweeb. I still track the computer industry and subscribe to the bible of the computer industry, *Byte* magazine. I am the master of my own computer and am oft-referred to as an expert. I can open up my computer and add memory or other new devices and understand all the little nuances of my system. But I'd rather read a good book than explore some hot new program. I'd rather play Monopoly with friends after a great dinner than play the new Monopoly CD-ROM game that allows you to link with others through the Internet.

That's not to say I don't use the power of the computer as a tool; I still believe it to be one of the most remarkable inventions ever. And I remain passionate in my belief that we should all learn to master the power that it offers us. I just don't think it should rule my life, so I am post-dweeb. I live life to the fullest, both in the computer world and outside of it. It's a good strategy to follow.

> **It's important that we look upon the purveyors of all this technology not as Internet freaks. We must see them as they are — pragmatic businessmen and women who are on the fast track to a new society.**
> "No More Turf Wars?" *International Business,* October, 1995

We need to be less insulting of those whom we do not fully comprehend. Words like geek, dweeb and nerd are, if you think about them, terribly insulting. But we use them with abandon and too often, use them to stereotype people.

I like to think that I'm a normal, average human being and simply one who has turned the tables on technology so that I take advantage of it, rather than having it the other way around. Yet I find that many times, when I am talking to a crowd or appear in the media, people tend to categorize me as a geek or a nerd. It's demeaning, insulting and really not fair. People will treat you as you treat them; hence changing your attitude towards the power user is a good way to get the best of their guidance, support and counsel.

14
The Promise of Technology

> *Many people imagined that by the year 1984 computers would dominate our lives. Prof. N. W. Thring envisioned a world with household robots, and B. F. Skinner forecast that teaching machines would be commonplace. Arthur L. Samuel, a Dartmouth conference attendee from IBM, suggested that computers would be capable of learning, conversing and translating language; he also predicted that computers would house our libraries and compose most of our music.*
>
> Stephanie Haack, "A Brief History of Artificial Intelligence," *in Digital Deli*, edited by Steve Ditlea (Workman Publishing, New York, 1984)

Some of you might remember *The Jetsons*, a popular TV show during the 1960s, and one that is still available in syndication today. Before *The Jetsons*, there was the movie *Forbidden Planet*, featuring Robbie the Robot. Other entertainment at the time featured all kinds of fancy new technological wonders. We found ourselves growing up with visions of a world made better through technology and a general belief that more technology was a good thing.

The Jetsons cartoon featured the twenty-first century family, simple folks who tried to cope with the ultimate, hi-tech wonder world. You remember the cast of characters:

• Rosie, the somewhat out-of-date robot — newer models being available — who always cleaned the house to shining perfection, all while moving around the house with her radio antenna ready to receive a new instruction.

> **Progress might have been all right once, but it has gone on too long.**
>
> Ogden Nash

• Jane, the wife, who could instantly prepare dinner — anything from pizza to five-course meals, simply by pressing a button in her ultra-modern space kitchen. She was a master of the technology and lived the ultimate leisurely lifestyle as a result.

• Elroy, the genius kid-nerd who had all the technology figured out. A straight-A student, he specialized in studying space history, astrophysics and star geometry.

• Judy, the daughter, who was stereotyped as the typical teenage girl of the 1960s, unfazed by the modern world in which she lived, instead concentrating her energies on clothes, dating, guys and having fun.

• And finally, the hapless George Jetson, a ne'er-do-well who never seemed to be able to deal with all the modern stuff around him and always made the wrong decisions — a rather old-fashioned fellow in a modern time!

The Jetson family lived in a home perched high in the sky and enjoyed every kind of modern, twenty-first century convenience. Life for them was simple and easy, since so much of the complexity had been removed by the marvels of technology.

Everyone traveled in flying cars some of the time and through special pneumatic tube elevators the rest. People didn't have to walk given the preponderance of automatic sidewalks. Clothes and dishes were cleaned by marvelous devices that didn't need water. Dogs were walked on special automatic treadmills. You never saw a tree!

Careers and work? They barely existed. George only worked three days a week, for two hours a day, at Spaceley Sprockets.

Even before the *The Jetsons,* a show that aired long before *Star Trek,* shared with us its view of the future, our generation and those before us lived in a world that was characterized by often glowing, wonderful predictions of the future.

The 1950s were a time of enchantment for many. Once the Second World War ended, life seemed full of promise. The automobile, jet travel and television opened our vistas beyond our own local city and town to the rest of the world. Modern conveniences such as the dishwasher entered our homes, freeing us from some of the drudgery of the day-to-day world. Promises of cheap electricity fueled by the power of the atom filled news reports.

> ...the fifties, an extraordinary decade. Never before had we delighted in such a rain of innovations with such an immediate and intimate effect on our daily lives. Television took root everywhere. The Polaroid camera, the aqualung, the transistor radio and the birth-control pill came on the market. The hi-fi and stereo industry sprang up. Commercial jet travel became standard. Polio was controlled. The hydrogen bomb, the ICBM, space satellites, and the computer were all significant public issues....In that atmosphere, no technological achievement seemed beyond us and no forecast too fantastic.
>
> Fred Hapgood, "Computers Aren't So Smart After All," *Atlantic Monthly*, August, 1974

It was an unparalleled time of promise and excitement, peaking in 1964 with the World's Fair in New York. With its "World of Tomorrow" exhibit, the Fair was used as a forum by industry to summarize their view that the future would be automatic, wonderful and easy, all because of the magic of all kinds of technology.

The A&T Videophone was on display! Moving sidewalks! Space travel! All kinds of wonderful inventions showing us the way to the future. And at the time, predictions from the corporate world echoed this sense of well-being in the future.

> In 1972 Goodyear's Industrial Products Division thought it had identified a growing market for moving sidewalks. Its "Speedwalk" or "Speedramp" system would be used to transport shoppers and strollers around downtown areas, where no cars would be allowed. The firm felt confident that this would be a $6-billion-a-year industry in the 1980s....Needless to say, moving sidewalks did not turn out to be a growth market at all. In fact, large cities like New York spend huge sums to ensure that heaving sidewalks caused by freezing and thawing will not move unexpectedly and injure their citizens.
>
> Steven P. Schnaars, *MEGAMISTAKES: Forecasting and the Myth of Rapid Technological Change* (The Free Press, a Division of Simon and Schuster, New York, 1989)

Looking back today, we must wonder whether entire research departments were watching *The Jetsons* for their day-to-day research or moonlighting as writers for the show. For example, scientists at General Electric spoke of the automated kitchen, with the combination of the microwave and freezer providing one-button cooking.

Elsewhere, terms such as "ultrasonic technology" entered the vocabulary, as both *Fortune* and the *Wall Street Journal* predicted in 1964 that we would soon have devices that would provide us with the ability for ultrasonic cleaning of dishes and clothes. *Newsweek* followed up with a prediction that within ten years we would find ourselves taking ultrasonic showers. All of which seemed to parallel devices used in *The Jetsons* in 1962 and 1963.

> **The assumption that more technology is automatically good is so ingrained in our thinking that it is hardly questioned.**
>
> Seen on the Internet

Predictions weren't restricted to home appliances: by 1972, Goodyear seemed to continue with the trend of taking a page from

The Jetsons, outlining that a new era of transportation would soon be upon us, based on the massive adoption of its moving sidewalk technology.

As for Rosie the robot, just wait, we were told. The media in the 1960s was full of news stories predicting the imminent arrival of personal robots for the home. The future wasn't just something to be found on cartoon shows!

> **...in 10 years, personal robots will be able to handle such routine domestic tasks as washing windows, making beds, and vacuuming floors.**
> Bernie E. Woller, "Energy Usage and Control in the Home of the Future," *Management Quarterly*, Winter, 1985/1986

The arrival of the computer occurred right in the middle of this early sense of technological excitement. Computers were heralded as a marvelous new invention: an electronic brain. In fact, the first popular book about computers, released in 1949, was entitled *Giant Brains, or Machines That Think*. So at the same time that we had all of these glowing reports about the role of ultrasonic technology and robots and other wonderful stuff, we were introduced to the wonderful promise of the computer, the electronic brain!

> **Tom Watson Jr, who had committed IBM's future to the computer — the paragon of automation — tried to calm the public fears: "A lot of these people call these machines giant brains and when I hear the term I shudder, because they are giant tools ... not giant brains, and if you have giant tools you're upgrading men not downgrading them."**
> Jon Palfreman and Doron Swade, *The Dream Machine — Exploring the Computer Age* (BBC Books, London, 1991)

We were led to believe that we were on the threshold of a new era of "thinking machines" that would be able to analyze and comprehend in a way that would soon exceed our own capabilities. Take a look at some of the early news reports:

- 100 ton brain at M.I.T., *Scholastic*, February 4, 1946

- For sale — electronic brains, *Newsweek*, April 5, 1948

- Want to buy a brain? *Popular Mechanics*, May, 1949

- Machines to do tomorrow's thinking, *Coronet*, November, 1950

- Robot brain: moron or genius? *Science Digest*, February, 1952

- Whirlwind One: Speediest electro-brain! *Science Digest*, March, 1952

- Magic brain services American airlines, *Flying*, October, 1952

- Will machines replace the human brain? *American Mercury*, January, 1953

- Do electronic brains really think? *Science Digest*, March, 1953

- Machines that think, *Reader's Digest*, February, 1954

Such reporting didn't end in the 1950s. Although the term "electronic brains" soon disappeared, stories continued about the ultimate arrival of computers that could think just like us. Even in the 1970s the enthusiasm continued: in June, 1973 the *Wall Street Journal* ran the story "Latest Machines See, Hear, Speak and Sing — and May Outthink Man."

Computers! They were machines that would be able to function just like us!

We grew up in a period when the computer establishment seemed to have some compelling need to cast the computer in our own image and desire to develop computers that were "alive." I've always wondered why. For example, when it came to robots, not only were predictions made that they would soon become common, but there were reports that they would contain an awesome degree of computerized intelligence that would make it difficult to distinguish them from us.

Newsweek made this observation in the October 24, 1960 article, "Machines are This Smart": "tomorrow will bring stranger and smarter robots that take dictation and type letters, draw blueprints, make medical diagonses, and as now seems likely, know how to reproduce themselves."

> **In the 1950s and 1960s, "a lot of effort was devoted to programs which played chess and checkers, found proofs for theorems in geometry and symbolic logic, composed music and poetry, simulated neuroses. There was even a psychiatry program...."**
> Fred Hapgood, "Computers Aren't So Smart After All," *Atlantic Monthly*, August, 1974

Such fancy was based on the explosion of research in the 1950s and 1960s into what quickly came to be called "artificial intelligence." Massive expenditures were invested, particularly by the U.S. military establishment, to develop these so-called thinking machines. Much of the effort at academic institutions at the time was being poured into so-called cognitive capabilities, with computers that could reason and understand logic just like us. That's why we saw so many computers that could play chess and checkers, prove a theorem or undertake a psychiatric analysis.

> **It seems that the phrase "water goat" kept cropping up in the translation of a Russian engineering paper until it was discovered that the words were the translation of the phrase "hydraulic ram."**
> "Machines are This Smart," *Newsweek*, October 24, 1960

Similarly, efforts were made to develop the capability by which computers could converse through the keyboard and by voice. One hot topic was translation software; with the heat of the Cold War, there was an identified need for a computer that could do Russian translation. Experts foresaw pocket-size devices that would instantly translate any language on the planet, just by listening in on a conversation. Early efforts were less than fruitful, with some rather abysmal results.

Machines would be able to learn all about you, by watching what you did, and would modify their activities accordingly. Machines — technology — would be made intelligent through the power of the computer.

There was a certain promise implicit in this technological fascination: intelligent machines would free us from the drudgery of work. We were destined to become the leisure society.

From the earliest arrival of computers on the scene, news coverage often took the angle that we would soon see the ultimate in job nirvana: the reduced work week. It was perceived that computers would be able to take on much of the effort that people put into the mundane things in life, whether that be with their job or with their personal lives. In the article "Why Work?" in *Newsweek*, February 12, 1962, a social psychologist had this observation: "In the home, husbands who work shorter hours will be around the house more than the kids are…[Donald A.] Michael darkly inquires: 'What will they do all their long lives, day after day, four-day weekend after four-day weekend, vacation after vacation…?'" The perception was that computers would simplify the world of business so much that we would suddenly find ourselves with too much leisure time on our hands.

> **Computers…would produce enormous amounts of enforced leisure time. In a BBC documentary in 1966, a spokesman for General Motors predicted: "by the year 1990 or so we will first of all delay the entry of the working force into the labour market, (and) people will start to go to work at about the age 25 … We also think the retirement age will be coming down and that probably on average, retirement will occur at about age 50. And in the 25 years that will constitute the working part of a man's life, he will work about half what he works today, that is, he will have six months' vacation a year, or if**

> he works an entire year at a 40-hours week, he will take next year off as a sabbatical year. I don't believe this is a pipe dream at all. I think this is merely a continuation of the trends that we've already seen in the last 50 years, and the impact the computer will have in mechanizing the white collar part of our economy."
>
> Jon Palfreman and Doron Swade, *The Dream Machine — Exploring the Computer Age* (BBC Books, London, 1991)

We would work for as little as one to two hours each day, or only two or three days a week. Leisure industries would boom, as we found ourselves freed from the shackles of work, ready to enjoy the fruit, the free time, provided by the computer revolution. Just like George Jetson, I suppose.

In retrospect, it all seems rather silly. In "Computers Aren't So Smart After All," an article which appeared in *Atlantic Monthly*, August, 1974, some questions were raised about the early excitement over the potential for computers. "Every culture has its juvenile embarrassments; misdirected enthusiasms which fail dramatically and in retrospect seem to say something humiliating about the civilization that pursued them. The great computer craze of the fifties and sixties is such a case." Clearly, the holy grail of computers — the robot, speech and artificial intelligence — has not been achieved. And most of us continue on with the five-day work week.

It took some time for the enthusiasm to disappear; you could even find reference to the topics in the 1970s. The respected publication *ComputerWorld*, long measuring the pulse of the computer industry, carried just such an article in its May 17, 1982 edition, titled "Human Race Predicted to Die in Favor of 'Living' Robots/Marry a Robot? Futurist Says Yes by Year 2000." "According to Arthur Harkins, director of the graduate program in futures research at the University of Minnesota, nonbiological entities created by humans will gradually replace humans. The key to this is the biochip, which is a semiliving, molecule-size neuron-equivalent circuit. Humans will be modified through a combination of genetic engineering and implants of artificial intelligence ... and artificial organs....Humans with special needs, such as burn victims, will "marry" robots by 2000, although such unions will not be legal marriages."

But eventually, sanity prevailed, with a gradual recognition by both the industry and society that perhaps the idea of "electronic brains" was too fanciful and too far-fetched.

Over time, glowing forecasts of a better future due to technology began to fade, as many of the predicted forecasts failed to come true. And our attitudes towards computer technology, and perhaps technology in general, suffer from the fact that maybe we have seen too many outlandish predictions that have not come true, particularly, computers that think, walk and talk. After all, growing up we were constantly exposed to a world that featured predictions about the marvelous impact of new technology, which, when they failed to deliver, engendered in us a skepticism that lingers to this day.

Forecasting the future — particularly with technology — is obviously a difficult thing to do. Many people have said that while it's easy to make a prediction about the future, it's another thing altogether to be right.

Consider, for example, one fellow who in 1868 tried to alert residents of London, England, that they would soon face a very serious problem. Why? In his studies, he had taken a look at the population growth rate of the city and then factored in the bathroom habits of the horses then used for travel. His conclusion? By 1968, most of London would be buried six feet deep in horse manure.

Why is it so difficult to predict the future? Can we determine how the wired world — the information age — is really going to evolve, given our past history of failed technological forecasts? It's a good question to consider.

It has been said that when it comes to computer technology, there are as many predictions for the future as there are computers. And some have observed that those who make the predictions do one of two things:

- they predict more of the same, or

- they make extremely outlandish predictions, so outlandish, in fact, that no one will remember what was said.

> Forecasters, it seems, are prone to see big changes when none are in store, and rapid changes when slower changes are more likely.
>
> These observations point up a common difference between successful and failed forecasts. The successes tend to be conservative in their outlook, while the failures foresee fantastic changes. The successes call for smaller, slower changes and reject radical innovations.
>
> Clearly, successful forecasts show a better sense of perspective. But, as (Nigel) Calder notes insightfully in his 1984 follow-up, "common sense is often smothered by special enthusiasm, selective inattention, political prejudice, wishful thinking, or doomsaying."
>
> Steven P. Schnaars, *MEGAMISTAKES: Forecasting and the Myth of Rapid Technological Change* (The Free Press, a Division of Simon and Schuster, New York, 1989).

The problem of properly forecasting the development and role of computer technology has long existed.

Early on, the problem was that people simply couldn't conceive what the machines might be used for. When the computer first arrived on the scene, the scientists involved in their development couldn't perceive that one day we would use them to play games, manage our home finances or converse with people on the other side of the world.

All of their energies centred around the belief that what they were developing was a giant calculator, designed specifically for the goal of assisting with the complex mathematical problems of the day involved in the fields of engineering and physics, such as atomic weapons.

> **If this new invention was merely an exceptionally fast arithmetic machine, it followed that the world would only ever need a few of them. After all, one machine could do the work of 10,000 human computers with calculators. In the post-war electronic era there were suggestions that Britain would need just three or four computers and the United States six at most.**
>
> Jon Palfreman and Doron Swade, *The Dream Machine — Exploring the Computer Age* (BBC Books, London, 1991)

If that was to be their role, they thought, then clearly there wouldn't be a lot of people who might need the sophisticated capabilities they provided. Perhaps a few research centres, here and there, around the world, that would be it!

Such attitudes might seem laughable today, but even those who were destined to play a major role in the future computer industry could not foresee the significance of what they developed. Thomas Watson, Sr., the head of IBM at the time, indicated in the early 1950s that he thought there might be a global market for perhaps six computers. Today, with over 150 million personal computers in the world, these predictions seem a tad off base.

The problem of technological forecasting doesn't exist solely with computer technology. And often people have been correct in their forecasts, but have been attacked nonetheless.

Robert Goddard, for example, now acknowledged as the father of the rocket engine, was ridiculed by none other than the *New York Times*, which, in a savage editorial, dismissed his invention as mere fancy and indicated that mankind would never master the heavens.

> **The best way to predict the future is to invent it.**
>
> Alan Kay

Such skepticism is abundant regardless of the invention. At a meeting of the Western Telegraph Company in 1906, one stockholder stated that the new "wireless telegraph" (radio) would not be a threat to the company. Western Union, of course, soon found that radio transmission did some fairly significant damage to its core business.

> Professor Richard Woolley, Astronomer Royal, stoutly declared in 1957 that "the future of interplanetary travel is utter bilge." He was in good company. As early as 1920 the *New York Times* had pointed out that rocket pioneer Robert Goddard "only seems to lack the knowledge ladled out daily in high schools," because he believed that a spacecraft would operate in a vacuum. As for flying to the moon, "the proposition appears to be basically impossible," observed Professor A.W. Bickerton in 1926. In 1936, J.P. Lockhart-Mummery clinched the argument: "The acceleration...from rockets...inevitably would damage the brain beyond repair."
> Cliff McGoon, "Predictions from a decade ago – Revisited," *Communication World*, January/February, 1994

Consider the advisor who told President Harry Truman in 1943 that the atomic bomb would never work, and that the entire project was foolhardy. Or the Engineer-in-Chief of the British Post Office, who in 1878 dismissed the idea of electric light, a proposition that looks particularly ludicrous today.

In 1902, *Harpers Weekly* dismissed the idea of dedicated roads for motor cars, which might have made sense at the time, since autos were only beginning to be used in their most experimental stages. Today, of course, such a prediction looks absolutely silly.

Often, the problem isn't that others dismiss the invention; sometimes even the inventor cannot possibly comprehend what the invention is good for. Just take a look at Thomas Edison. When he invented the phonograph, he couldn't pinpoint the key use for it, instead believing that it would be used for many other things. Clearly, technological forecasting is a significant challenge.

> Another interesting characteristic of technology evolution is that the immediate use, and even the potential long-term use, of a new invention is difficult to determine. And the inventor himself is often the worst spokesperson for its potential uses.

> Thomas Edison, for example, published an article in 1878 describing [several] ways that the phonograph might prove useful to the public:
> Taking dictation without the aid of a stenographer
> Providing "talking books" for the blind
> Teaching public speaking
> Reproducing music
> Preserving important family sayings, reminiscences and the last words of the dying
> Creating new sounds of music boxes and musical toys
> Preserving the exact pronunciation of foreign languages
> Teaching spelling and other rote material
> Recording telephone calls
>> Notice that "taking dictation" was first on the list, but musical reproduction was only fourth; many of the other suggested applications look ludicrous to us a century later.
>
> Edward Yourdon, *Decline and Fall of the American Programmer* (Prentice Hall, Englewood Cliffs, New Jersey, 1992)

Why does the future not turn out like predicted, particularly when it comes to computer technology? To find out the answer, I turned to the book *MEGAMISTAKES: Forecasting and the Myth of Rapid Technological Change* (The Free Press, a division of Simon and Schuster, New York, 1989). It is a book that takes an in-depth look at predictions that have been made through time about technology and examines why the predictions are so far off the mark.

The main conclusion? All too often, those responsible for making the prediction are so directly involved with the technology that they cannot think straight! Put another way, they are far too in "love" with the technology to be rational! Notes author Steven P. Schnaars, "the forecasters who construct them are blinded by their emotions and lose perspective of commonsense economic consideration. They are swept away. They incorrectly assume

> **Isn't it interesting that the same people who laugh at science fiction listen to weather forecasts and economists.**
>
> Kelvin Throop, III

that consumers will find the new technology as enticing and irresistible as they do. In most instances, those assumptions are very wrong."

When it comes to computers, the problem is rampant. One need only look to the predicted "paperless office" and the oft-made statements by the computer industry that we are finally on the verge of seeing a reduction in the use of paper. It's certainly not an old belief; as far back as October, 1955 there was an article in *Fortune* headlined "Coming Victory Over Paper."

I don't know about you, but I certainly find that when I visit an office, there seems to be a heck of a lot of paper about. Yet another computer promise bites the dust!

Not only have we grown up with a skepticism about technology and computers due to failed forecasts, but we have developed a sense of suspicion and fear about its impact.

It's clear that we had a sense of wonder in the 1950s and 1960s when it came to technology, but soon we began to encounter the darker side of what technology could do when we were introduced to HAL, the computer in the movie *2001: A Space Odyssey*. Here at last, in the midst of the uproar and confusion that surrounded us in the 1960s, we had the perfect understanding of what a computer could be. It would be a faithful tool, with a level of intelligence on par with humans, if not exceeding them. It could speak, think and play a mean game of chess. The voice of HAL was soothing, relaxing and about as conversant as any other person.

The "computer as a life form" image was complete! HAL didn't seem like a machine; rather, "he" was a partner on the voyage, strong, knowing and ever-present. So while watching the movie, we were at first reassured and fascinated. The future role of the computer in our lives could be quite positive, after all! Or so we thought.

As *2001: A Space Odyssey* progressed, we became aware of an evil side to HAL; at the same time that "he" was smart, he was evil, to the extent that he was capable of committing the ultimate act of murder. We were stunned! Computers might not be simple electronic brains, about to deliver us into a world of the shortened work week! Instead, they could be evil, nasty devices, technology gone amuck!

> **The sixties was a decade in which apprehensions about the effects of technology became widespread, and glittering inventions ceased to enhance our daily lives.**
> Fred Hapgood, "Computers Aren't So Smart After All," *Atlantic Monthly*, August, 1974

Looking back, we can see that the duplicity of HAL heralded a new era, one that involved a changing attitude towards technology. It wasn't just HAL but many other things, perhaps most importantly, what we witnessed with the horror of technology gone mad in the Vietnam war. We became skeptical of the wonders of technology in general.

Ralph Nader entered our consciousness, with his indications that something was wrong with the technology of the world. And over time, the future held for us not the exciting glow of wonderful technology but of nuclear plant meltdowns at Chernobyl and Three Mile Island. We saw the *Apollo 1* mission burn on the pad with the loss of three lives and sat in terrorized silence when *Challenger* exploded in the sky.

We became skeptical of the benefits of all of this new technology and began to challenge the views of the scientists who pronounced it to be good.

There is a lesson to be learned from all of this: our attitude towards technology will always be one of enthusiasm balanced by skepticism. Of course, we can look at predictions from the past and snicker. How foolish they were! How incorrect were their predictions! How silly their anticipated future!

Even today, as predictions continue to be made about the fabulous role of computer technology, such as virtual reality, the "information superhighway" and other topics, we aren't quite sure if we should believe all of them. Our ingrained skepticism, our built-in disbelief of the benefit and role of technology, blinds us to the potential impact of such new technological developments.

We are held hostage by our exposure to the future of yesterday and the reality of too many promises of the past that remain unfulfilled. How can we believe what is promised today?

Given the shaky state of accuracy found with predictions of the future and our deep-seated negative attitude towards technology, it's important that you learn how to manage your own attitudes when you hear about the impact of some hot new computer technology.

> **Of all the technologies we have invented, the computer has been the most difficult to interpret and predict. Forty years ago scientists sincerely believed that the world would need only a handful of computers. Will the uses to which we are putting computers seem similarly naïve 40 years from now?**
> Jon Palfreman and Doron Swade, *The Dream Machine — Exploring the Computer Age* (BBC Books, London, 1991)

Let's face it. One challenge that you have likely had in your struggle with technology is that you don't feel "with it." You often feel left behind and that so many other people are marching further ahead than you in their capabilities. But much of this might be due to the fact that they are all too willing to accept the amazing and awesome predictions that surround them. My attitude?

1. The willingness to believe the future, combined with a healthy skepticism about what you hear, is the best approach to staying "with it."

2. Recognize that for a long time we have been dealing with developers in the computer industry who all too often get carried away with their beliefs of how significant and wonderful their new invention is. Their beliefs often do not turn out to be correct; something else does!

3. Learn to carefully analyze the excessive and amazing levels of hype that surround some new development with computers, before you conclude that you are falling behind!

4. Do not be suspicious of everything as a result of our being misguided. Because we were continually encouraged to believe that computers would instantly lead to positive and dramatic change in our life, our suspicions grew when they did not.

5. Feel safe to ignore the "holy triad" of the computer revolution: artificial intelligence, computers that talk and robots! Someday technology will be able to do these things, but probably not in our lifetime. Computers never evolve according to the dreams of those who develop them.

6. Keep your mind open to all the new developments; otherwise, you will fall into complacency and continue to think that tomorrow will be much like it is today.

Arthur C. Clarke, the author of *2001: A Space Odyssey* and many other science fiction books, perhaps said it best: "all attempts to predict the future in any detail appear ludicrous within a few years." It's good to keep an open mind.

15

A Question of Trust

> *To err is human, but to really foul things up requires a computer.*
>
> Farmer's Almanac, 1978

Many of the youth of today have come to accept the wonder and passion of the information age. They readily accept that computers are a technology that can improve both their working and personal lives. They don't spend much time questioning the role of the technology. But we do, because at the same time that we began to lose our fascination with the technological world due to the failed promises of what it would deliver, we discovered that computers can make mistakes. Big ones.

We have lived in the era of the computer gone mad. Or so it often seems.

We knew that HAL the computer went insane and killed the crew, and we knew that something wasn't right with this marvelous new technology. And around the same time that we began to question the basic tenet that more technology is a good thing, we started to hear real stories of the strange things that these machines could do.

> In many a U.S. household last week, the story was the same. The morning mail had brought a bill for a charge-account or credit-card purchase, and in one way or another something was wrong. The customer was charged for something he had never bought. The amount was double what it should have been. The bill had been paid months ago. The common reaction: rage, often followed by helpless frustration…
>
> "The Great Snafu," *Newsweek*, September 15, 1969

It might have happened to our parents or perhaps friends of the family. We might have read about it in the newspaper or saw reports on television. We heard people talk about it at parties and saw comedians make jokes about it on late night shows.

It went like this: every once in a while we would see a photograph in the newspaper of a lady or a man holding up a stack of paper. The headline announced that some type of massive billing mistake had been made and that the customer had received a credit card, hydro or telephone bill for *several millions of dollars*. The person in the photo, the victim of a crazy computer somewhere, looked bemused, as if to say, isn't this funny?

But other stories of computer foul-ups began to appear, mistakes that didn't involve just billing systems. All of them seemed terribly amusing, unless they happened to us. Drivers were pulled over — and sometimes dragged off to jail — because the police computer confused them with someone else. There were 2-year-olds and dogs and cats and even fish who received credit cards, because a computer thought they were eligible. Students had their grades fouled up or found they couldn't register in a particular class because a computer made a mistake.

Some people were even pronounced to be dead by a computer system somewhere and were forced to fight a lively battle to prove that it was not so. As noted by Jon Palfreman and Doron Swade in the book *The Dream Machine — Exploring the Computer Age* (BBC

Books, London, 1991), "when mistakes occur they can prove difficult to correct. One story was cited in the *Los Angeles Times* of a man, Forman Brown, who a network (by mistake) thought was dead. His checks started coming back to him with the words "deceased" stamped on them. His problem spread to the Social Security Office which didn't want to pay his State Pension and to Medicare, who refused to reimburse him for doctors' bills incurred after he had officially died."

Tales of woe and error began to invade our consciousness. And clearly, our understanding of these machines began to be tarnished by the stories that we heard.

For many, the first thing that seemed to go wrong was a problem with their credit cards. There was no doubt that the computer was the fuel for the explosion in the use of charge cards in the 1950s and 1960s. Their arrival meant that companies could finally build the sophisticated systems necessary to manage massive volumes of credit card transaction information. But at the same time that computers permitted this new form of transaction, they were relatively new to the world of business, and executives and companies were only beginning to learn what it would take to implement them. Often, simple but far-reaching mistakes were made that had disastrous effects. It was like mixing oil and water: the combination of inexperience and new technology just was not meant to be, and thus began the era of the charge card foul-up.

> One of the tales you might hear at a party goes like this: A woman gets a bill from her credit card company for zero dollars and zero cents. She laughs and tosses it in the trash. Two weeks later she gets another bill from the company for zero dollars and zero cents, with a computerized form letter urging her to pay up. She shrugs and tosses that. Two weeks pass and she gets the same bill for $0.00, with a nasty form letter telling her [that her] credit will be ruined if she doesn't pay up.

> **So she writes out a cheque for zero dollars and zero cents, sends it in, and never hears from the computer again.**
>
> Karla Jennings, *THE DEVOURING FUNGUS: Tales of the Computer Age*
> (W.W. Norton & Company, New York, 1990)

So many people started to get charge card bills that were so obviously in error that *Newsweek* was prompted to write the article "The Great Snafu" in 1969. The article was typical of the time; it noted how one fellow kept receiving past-due notices for $0.00. He ignored them, until one day he sent a cheque to the company for that amount in order to keep the computer happy. And the same article mentioned the story of another lady who discovered to her horror that every time she bought something, the amount charged on her credit card was double the actual purchase.

> **The major difference between a thing that might go wrong and a thing that cannot possibly go wrong is that when a thing that cannot possibly go wrong goes wrong, it usually turns out to be impossible to get at and repair.**
>
> Douglas Adams

The problems seemed to be several: errors in amounts that were billed, payments that were never credited, and charges that were never reversed. Woe seemed to befall anyone who had a charge card, and news reports of credit card foul-ups began to dominate much of the coverage of computers in the mid- to late 1960s.

Certainly we were now beyond news stories of computers as "electronic brains" and into the era of computers as giant mistakes!

A sense of distrust descended upon the population. Not only did the fictional HAL of the movie theatre go mad, but the actual computers of the day were insane!

Discussion about computer foul-ups began to enter day-to-day conversation, as people related the latest story of horror, often with bemusement, but more often than not with disbelief. The fact that computers were making so many mistakes began to dominate discussions at parties, business meetings and at family get-togethers. The electronic brains of the world were going crazy!

> **Dear Ann,**
> **I think I can top the person who wrote complaining about the idiocy of the phone company. Talk about garbage in, garbage out!**
> **When AT&T split with Bell, we had three phones in our house. The equipment belonged to Ma Bell and the service belonged to AT&T. After we returned all the phone equipment to Ma Bell, we received a bill for $0.00. A few weeks later, we received a check for $5 and a note thanking us. Several months later, we received another computerized bill for $0.00. We called again, got nowhere, so we sent another check for $0.00. A few weeks later we received another $5 refund with the same thank you.**
> **This went on every three months for two years. Now we are down to once a year and have given up trying to straighten this out. We just cash the $5 and forget about it.**
>
> Linda K.R. in California, Ann Landers column, *Providence RI Journal*, July 1, 1987

And the sad reality is that news coverage of computers making mistakes has stayed with us well into the 1980s and 1990s, as efforts to tame the wild beast continue. In many ways, the problems have never disappeared, nor has our frustration with computers gone mad.

As we moved into the 1970s and 1980s, more news reports began to focus on other types of computer failure, and society began to pick up on the fact that these machines were not infallible. The term "computer bug" gained prominence; it was an all-purpose way to describe what had gone wrong with a computer system somewhere.

It was during this time that computer technology began to invade other technologies: everything from our toaster ovens to the automobiles we drove to the planes we flew in. And as their presence expanded in the ever-expanding technological world, we began to hear of all kinds of additional things that could go wrong.

> **We are living the events which for centuries to come will be minutely studied by scholars who will undoubtedly describe these days as probably the most exciting and creative in the history of mankind. But preoccupied with our daily chores, our worries and personal hopes and ambitions, few of us are actually living in the present.**
> Lawrence K. Frank

For a long time, a group of computer scientists that calls itself the Association for Computing Machinery has tracked some of the more bizarre and prominent failures to occur since the 1960s as the technological society came to place ever-increasing reliance on the power of the computer. Their stories are available on the Internet today. Reading them provides fascinating insight into technology that had really gone wrong.

> **In 1988, owners of some GM Chevrolet Astro and GMC Safari vans were advised that the rotten egg smell coming from their vehicles was the fault of a computer! It turns out that the fault was with a computer that monitors the fuel mix for the vehicles.**
> Seen on the Internet

- Computers began to be used within automobiles, with sometimes disastrous results. A bug in the computer brake system of El Dorado automobiles resulted in a massive recall, while 14,000 Ford Lincolns were recalled when a computer problem in the air suspension system led to an overheating problem, sometimes causing the car to burst into flames. Other problems emerged with fuel emission and other systems, as computers took over responsibility for the monitoring of engine and vehicle performance.

- The space program was in a large part made possible because of computer technology, but it was not without its share of problems; there were any number of launches that we saw delayed or scrubbed as the result of a "computer error." In fact, some errors were more real and severe than others: the *Mariner 1* unmanned launch to Mars failed in 1962 due to the use of a period instead of a comma in a computer program. And another *Mariner* space probe was lost due to one missing word in a computer program. And although it wasn't widely reported, in the last few minutes before *Apollo 11* landed on the moon, a computer alarm buzzed mercilessly, distracting the crew and almost causing the mission to be aborted. The problem? The computer was overloaded with data; it couldn't cope.

• The aeronautics industry quickly grabbed onto the reigns of the computer revolution sweeping the world, as computers were implemented within passenger and military aircraft. There are stories that the original F16 jet autopilot system had the nasty tendency of flipping the plane upside down whenever it crossed the equator, due to a misguided computer instruction. And an F14 jet once flew off the end of an aircraft carrier by accident, directly into the North Sea, because of a software error. And there are plane crashes attributable to computers, such as an Air New Zealand crash in Antarctica in 1979, where the on-board computer detected an error but did not inform the crew.

• Severe financial system problems emerged, which were a little more serious than simple billing problems, as the economic engine of the world's banking system came to rely on computer-based transactions. One high-profile story involved a computer error in 1985 which almost resulted in disaster for the financial markets, a situation that actually did occur with the stock market crash of 1987. In that year, stock prices were subject to havoc, when computers automatically began to bail out of the market without human intervention.

• The defence systems that ostensibly protected us during the Cold War were gradually computerized. News reports terrified us with their scenarios so similar to the movie *Dr. Strangelove*, in which nuclear war could start as the result of some type of accident, perhaps a computer accident. Indeed it almost did. There is the story that at one point, the NORAD defence radar system computer mistook the moon for a hostile incoming missile and another error in which a Soviet test missile was detected as being aimed at Hamburg, Germany, instead of the Arctic.

> **In 1985, a computer malfunction at the Bank of New York almost brought financial havoc to global financial markets. The problem was overcome only when the Federal Reserve Bank provided $20 billion to the bank to help it get around the temporary foul-up — a $32 billion overdraft!**
> Seen on the Internet

• Other military systems came to rely on the computer, often with the result of the direct loss of human life. It is said that during the Falklands War, the *HMS Sheffield* radar system identified an incoming Argentinean missile as friendly, since it was non-Soviet, with the resultant loss of many lives. The missile wasn't Soviet; the Argentineans bought it from the French.

• Then there are the numerous breakdowns we have seen with telephone, telecommunication, air traffic control and other systems. Large-scale failures, in which entire systems came crashing down due to a computer error, such as in 1979, when a software problem knocked out all long distance phone service to Greece, or the major AT&T failure of 1991, which saw a large portion of the telephone system in the United States come to a crashing halt.

• As the medical profession came to rely on computers, horrifying stories emerged of software bugs in medical devices, the result of which led to the deaths of patients due to massive exposure to radiation. In an article "Man killed by accident with medical radiation," in the *Boston Globe*, June 20, 1986, it was said that "a series of accidental radiation overdoses from identical cancer therapy machines in Texas and Georgia has left one person dead and two others with deep burns and partial paralysis, according to federal investigators. Evidently caused by a flaw in the computer program controlling the highly automated devices, the overdoses — unreported until now — are believed to be the worst medical radiation accidents to date. The defect in the machines was a "bug" so subtle, say those familiar with the cases, that although the accident occurred in June 1985, the problem remained a mystery until the third, most serious accident occurred on April 11 of this year."

And through all of this terror, the humorous side of computers has continued, unabated, with reports of individuals encountering any number of unique problems, including being swept out to sea. Take, for example, the correction notice which appeared in *The Canberra Times*, February 3, 1988: "For some considerable time, *The Canberra Times* has been publishing the wrong tide times for Narooma. The error has been in arithmetical calculation in this office of the difference between tide times at Fort Denison as published in standard tide tables and times at Narooma. The error, the source of which is lost in antiquity, was discovered last week when the editor, relying on *The Canberra Times* figures, was swept out to sea. But he managed to return to shore — and ordered this correction."

The message to us over the last 30 years has been clear and consistent: computers are inherently unstable, unreliable and untrustworthy. That they are should come as no surprise. After all, they simply mirror the frailties of the humans who created them.

The impact of growing up in an era in which computers made an ever-increasing number of mistakes was that we soon came to a quick conclusion because of these news stories: computers could not be trusted, since they happened to regularly make mistakes. To us, they seemed to be the ultimate Orwellian and bureaucratic nightmare and were but one more technology in a technological world gone mad.

> **A retired couple got a jolt from their July electric bill — $5,062,599.57 U.S. An offer by Tampa Electric Co. for them to pay "budget" monthly installments of $62,582.27 didn't help. Company officials apologized to Jim and Winnie Schoelkopf after the mistake was blamed on a computer operator. The correct bill was for $146.76.**
>
> Toronto Star, July 29, 1988

What bothered many people in the 1960s as billing problems emerged — a feeling that lingers to this day — was the attitude of the companies who were implementing the technology. Computer-generated billing notices often threatened to cut off credit, hydro or telephone services if the bill was not immediately paid. It didn't matter if the bill was for $10 or $10,000,000; if it was overdue, service would be terminated! After all, the computer was correct!

Letters accompanying such bills, most often automatically prepared by computer, were often threatening, impolite, nasty and impersonal. We found ourselves locked in battle with the machine, and the machine seemed to hold all the cards. People began to scream for help.

Public hysteria? Not quite, but it quickly got to the point that even *Reader's Digest* joined the fray, providing guidance to average folks in an article entitled "If a Computer Fouls Up Your Charge Account," in January, 1971. "Why do so many errors occur?" questioned the author. "Is there some way to keep computers from mangling your account? What can you do to extricate yourself from these bill imbroglios?"

> **Unfortunately, any charge account is going to get out of whack once in a while...the error can be relentlessly carried forward month after month until finally you begin receiving "collection letters," warning that your credit will be endangered or that you will become subject to legal action....**
>
> "If a Computer Fouls Up Your Charge Account," *Reader's Digest*, condensed from "Changing Times," *The Kiplinger Magazine*, January, 1971

The fact that *Reader's Digest* printed an article to help people deal with the problem of computer errors is instructive. With thousands of exasperated people beginning to experience frustration with new computerized credit card systems that did nothing but make mistakes, it was time for a leading publication to offer practical advice on how to deal with the problems once they had begun to occur.

But that article echoed the prevailing sentiment: the computer systems of the day seemed to dig in their heels and refuse to correct mistakes. The article even suggested that if legal action seemed imminent over an unpaid bill that was in error, then the CEO of the company should be contacted!

A feeling of helplessness spread across the land, as the impact of computer systems became clear. The experience led to a typical reaction: a wish for the future to slow down. The computer age meant that humanity itself — reason, emotion and simple conversation — were beginning to disappear. You couldn't solve your problem with a person; you had to deal with the machine!

Noted *Newsweek* in its Great Snafu article: "Many lament the old days when they were well known at stores and could straighten out billing errors with a simple friendly phone call." (These people, of course, had not yet encountered the joys of voice mail!)

Soon much of the social commentary at the time focused on — no, bemoaned is a better term — the ever-increasing lack of human contact in the relationship between the consumer and business. The message was clear: not only were computers untrustworthy, but we couldn't fight back!

Officials in the business world didn't help the situation any. Many executives in the 1960s were enamored with the machines; they could solve so many business problems! And all too often, they did not realize the extent of the problems that were unfolding. They were so in love with the technology and everything that it could do, that they could not see the problems that were occurring.

> **As far as we know, our computer has never had an undetected error.**
> Seen on the Internet

So the general public found they had to deal with company officials who were cold-hearted, bureaucratic and unwavering in their attitude. If you complained to a company, the answer came back that "if the computer had said it, it must be correct." People were forced to fight to have mistakes corrected, a ludicrous situation at best.

Today, of course, business has been humbled, even as computer-generated errors continue to occur, though perhaps not as frequently.

Companies now struggle mightily to put in place quality control procedures to ensure that their systems do not foul up. Great expenditures are made to test new systems before they go "live." Company officials are quick to respond to customers who seem to have a problem and seem to have come to accept that in many cases their systems are at fault.

> **...far from simplifying technology or business, the computer has added complexity and imposed a constantly changing set of demands on scientists and managers. The integration of a mishmash of computer functions into a smooth-running system has turned out to be more difficult than anyone, including computer makers, ever expected.**
> "The recession forces a reappraisal," *Business Week*, June 5, 1971

But these early days and experiences have tarnished our own understanding of computers. We grew up in a time in which the world of business was discovering the magic of the computer at the same time that it was oblivious to the frailties of their implementation, with the result that we have a deeply rooted distrust of what they do. A situation made worse by the next step in the evolution of computers: the introduction into our lexicon of the phrase "it's the computer's fault!"

A Question of Trust

What does all of this have to do with you? I think that many in our generation have developed a distrust of the technology. We've seen too many mistakes made and too many problems occur when the technology is misapplied. And so the potential unreliability of computers seems to be generally accepted by most people today. We fly, drive, work, play and live with technology that is based on the ubiquitous logic and functioning of the computer chip. And for all the ways in which the computer is used throughout our world, the occurrence of failure of the technology is actually quite low; things are not as bad as they seem.

> **If you look for the positive things in life, you will find them.**
>
> Unknown

But as adults, we are perhaps a little too stressed by the fact that *things can go wrong with computers*. We tend to focus on the negative aspects of these machines and close our minds to the fact that overall, reliability has actually become quite high.

Kids seem to approach computers differently; they seem to instinctively know that things will go wrong as they learn to use them and to explore them. If they are working with new software or are exploring a new computer system and something goes wrong, they simply turn off the power and start it again. They aren't fazed by unreliability.

> **Children have neither a past nor a future. Thus they enjoy the present — which seldom happens to us.**
>
> Jean De La Bruyere

Yet when I help out those in my generation, I see a different attitude. Unreliability, the fact that things might break, concerns us greatly. "But I might break it," seems to be a phrase that is all too acceptable. And because of the fear that we might "break it," we hold ourselves back from learning and exploring.

Once again, our situation is unique: we grew up amidst the hype and the promises of the electronic brain and didn't at first hear about the potential problems and challenges of computer technology. It was only through the horror stories — sometimes sensationalized — that we heard in the media that we became aware of the fact that things can go wrong. And we can't deny that our attitudes have been affected as a result.

Perhaps that is one reason we are so nervous of that innocent little personal home computer that we bought. We glance at it as it sits over there in the corner, unloved, unwanted, because we are scared that if we try to learn it, we'll break it.

My advice? So what! What's wrong if you try something out and it doesn't work? Why are you so stressed about this possibility? Who cares if something breaks? Pick up the pieces and start again! Computers will break. Things will go wrong. Murphy's Law will kick in. Whatever the case may be, come to accept the potential fragility of what you are dealing with.

It's a pretty fundamental issue, and you might as well address it head-on:

1. As you continue to master the machine, expect that your own experiences will echo this reality; things will go wrong. Computers are subject to Murphy's Law.

2. Perhaps we have come to expect a state of perfection from technology that simply doesn't exist. We shouldn't.

And above all? Have a sense of humour! When something goes wrong with a computer — an inevitability — laugh about it, rather than letting it be a source of stress and frustration.

16

Computers and Humility

If builders built buildings the way programmers wrote programs, then the first woodpecker that came along would destroy civilization.

Seen on the Internet

In the mid-1980s, Ronald Reagan announced a program that came to be known as SDI, the Strategic Defense Initiative. Tension with what was then the Soviet Union was still running high at the time. As a way out of the ongoing arms race, a time in which each country deployed more and more nuclear missiles, Reagan proposed that the United States should instead establish a sophisticated defence system that would prevent Soviet missiles from inflicting nuclear damage on the United States. The Pentagon was firmly and squarely behind the proposal, believing that this would be the ultimate solution to an entirely vexing problem.

SDI would be based upon earth-orbiting satellites, each armed and programmed with sophisticated laser technology that would shoot any threatening missile launches. The heart of the system lay in to-be-developed computer technology that would be able to instantly recognize and identify any incoming missiles.

Reagan and the defence establishment passionately believed that only by erecting an impregnable shield of defence would the United States be able to forever protect itself from the Red Menace. And therein began one of the most fascinating debates in the history of computers, one that would eventually see most leading computer scientists come clearly down on the side of the argument that computers could never be made to be so reliable.

I learned about the human-computer interaction with a situation involving a house fire. Late one February night in the winter of 1993, we had retired early. I was just drifting off to sleep when my wife screamed, "Fire! Across the street!" Jumping out of bed, I scrambled for my glasses and ran to the window. One of the homes across the street was engulfed in flames. Some people milled about on the street, watching, silent in their horror. There were some screams as people grasped the site in front of them.

I threw on some clothes, a coat and shoes and ran outside. I quickly found another neighbour and began to ask him some frantic questions. One of which was, where the heck is the fire department? They were nowhere to be seen! It seemed an eternity — five minutes, maybe ten — before we heard the wail of the sirens and the rumble of their engines as they tore onto the street. Too late — the place was destroyed, fortunately without the loss of life.

The day after, the story emerged that the woman who lived in the house ran to the neighbours next door for help as soon as the fire started, who immediately called 911, stressing the seriousness of the situation. The dispatcher who took the call obtained the details and confirmed that trucks would be sent immediately.

But five minutes later, with the fire raging out of control and no sign of the fire department, my neighbours called 911 again. They were reassured that the trucks were on the way. Five minutes later they called again, with similar reassurances.

It took some 15 to 20 minutes for the fire trucks to arrive, and by that time, they could do little but pour water on the smoldering ruins.

What happened? It turned out that the dispatcher took the address from my neighbour, punching the name of our street into the computer system. Now, the name of our street is similar to that of another, and that other street *came up first on the computer screen*. Our street was listed second.

We heard that the dispatcher, after typing in the street name, pressed "Enter" on that first street address, thus causing the trucks to actually be dispatched to the wrong street, which was six kilometres away. It was only upon arriving there that the fire crew obviously saw that there was no fire, and called pleadingly into dispatch, only to find out that the problem was very far away.

I look at that home even today as an example of what can go wrong in the unique relationship between humans and machine, in that we could blame the situation on the clear lack of perfection in the way that people and computers interact.

We would do well, in managing our attitudes towards the computer, by coming to accept that their fragility merely mirrors the human condition. Computers are only as good as the people who program and operate them, and we all know that people make many mistakes. Computers simply do a wonderful job at abetting and compounding those mistakes.

To make no mistakes is not in the power of man; but from their errors and mistakes the wise and good learn wisdom for the future

Plutarch

Computer errors and mistakes come about in two ways. First, the folks who write computer programs can make mistakes, which we call bugs, that have a minor or sometimes major and dreadful impact. Second, the people who use and operate computers, whether they be bug-free or not, can make mistakes in the way they use them.

> **A C.R. Griffin spent a night in jail in Fairbanks, Alaska. The reason? The Department of Motor Vehicles computer indicated his license was suspended. The reality? The computer was supposed to check only the last two years of driving infractions, but the programmer made a mistake, resulting in it checking the last five years.**
>
> "DMV computer error puts innocent motorist in jail," *Computerworld*, April, 1985

It is the combination of those two points — the frailty of programming itself and things that can go wrong in their operation — that has led to the horror stories of the past and present involving billing system errors, failed rocket launches and fights with your local auto-licencing department. We are in the early stages of a world in which we and computers will increasingly interact, and there is a lot of learning underway as people try to learn how to increase and enhance the reliability of their operation and the way in which we interact with them. Mistakes are made in programming the computer, but they often are also made in the way that people interact with the machine.

There are no real computer errors; there are only errors made by people telling computers what to do and in the way that people use those machines. And people make a lot of mistakes. So if you ask a computer techie a question about some type of problem, you often get the reply, "it's not supposed to do that..." It isn't, but it does.

> **I heard the following tale on KCBS this morning. (I intersperse a few details from the SF Chron, 23 Jun 86.)**
> **It seems that this fellow Robert Barbour desired personalized license plates for his car. Since he loved sailing, he applied for "SAILING" and "BOATING" as his first two choices [seven years ago]. He couldn't think of a third name of NAUTICAL intent, so he wrote "NO PLATE" in as his third choice.**
> **You guessed it. He got "NO PLATE."**
> **A week or so later, he received his first parking ticket in the mail. This was followed by more and more tickets, from all over the state [2500 in all!]. It seems that when a police**

> officer writes a parking ticket for a car with no license plates, he writes "NO PLATE" on the ticket.
>
> Our friend took his problem to the DMV, which informed him that he should change his plates.
>
> The DMV also changed their procedures. They now instruct officers to write the word "NONE" on the unplated parking tickets.
>
> Wonder who's gonna get those tickets now?
>
> Posted on the Internet

Computers have awesome capabilities but they have no logic or emotion. They cannot tell right from wrong. They don't have a heck of a lot of common sense. And in preparing a computer program, it is often impossible to comprehend all the possible situations that might result.

What does this have to do with the Strategic Defense Initiative? When that debate began, it essentially caused the computer industry to focus upon the issue of reliability. When Reagan introduced the idea for SDI, there was a firestorm of debate within the global computing community, with those who believed it would be possible pitted against those who were convinced it to be folly.

The stakes were potentially very high. The system would have to work at 100% effectiveness; after all, if one nuclear missile got through the "shield," millions of lives would be lost. And over time, a consensus emerged. Leading computer scientists of the day refused to accept that SDI would be possible. They stated, unequivocally and without shame or concern, that computers could never be built to such a highly reliable degree. Software could never be made to be that reliable. Mankind would never be able to provide for 100% effectiveness. Things would go wrong. Mistakes would be made.

To me, that remains a startling and realistic admission that we would do well to recognize. Computers will always screw up. Remember that there are no computer errors, only human errors. So why be stressed about it? After all, how many perfect human beings do you know?

17

Closing Our Minds to the Possibilities

*I can't understand why people are frightened of new ideas.
I'm frightened of the old ones.*

John Cage

Remember the adage, life is like half a glass of water; some people see it as half empty and some see it as half full? I think that people who see the glass as half empty are also pessimistic about the information age, always looking for the negative aspects first. Personally, I always try to look for the positive aspects first. This makes looking at something new a lot easier.

I regularly encounter people who have convinced themselves that the information age is a terrible thing, and I have come to realize that they aren't really listening to what is being said. For instance, in November of 1996, I was being interviewed on a national radio show on the topic of personal finances. I was explaining for my host, a well-known Canadian financial personality, my belief that those of us who have mastered the information age can make better financial decisions as a result of having taught ourselves how to be better informed about the topic.

> ...I tell my audiences that 80 per cent of the things we see and think about are negative...
> And I say there's no reason to be this way when there is such opportunity within each of us to be the most passionately positive people anywhere in the world.
>
> Peter Legge, *You Can If You Believe You Can* (Eaglet Publishing, Burnaby, B.C., 1995)

This is a subject that is dear to my heart; I've written a book that explains how we can use the power of the Internet to better manage our personal financial affairs. The example I used for the radio listeners was that today's technology allows us to easily and quickly find comparative auto loan rates for all kinds of Canadian financial institutions. To me, this is a powerful capability; knowing what other banks offer will help you to negotiate a better deal with your bank manager. We spoke about online banking, comparative mortgage shopping online and how to make better investment decisions by researching information.

It was a phone-in show, and we took a lot of calls. Within minutes, one gentleman called in, and from the outset it was obvious that he wanted to take me to task. His comments centred around his belief that the whole world of online financial services was simply a waste of time, stupid and unnecessary. Not only that, but it would mean that bank branches would shut down, causing all kinds of people to lose their jobs.

To paraphrase, he said to me, "Guys like you really bug me. You are running around telling me that I won't use banks anymore and that we are going to do everything with computers and I think it is just plain dumb."

> **I was going to buy a copy of *The Power of Positive Thinking*, and then I thought: What the hell good would that do?**
>
> Ronnie Shakes

Listening to him, I realized that he had convinced himself that the message I was spreading was that banks would disappear as we rush off to the new financial computer age! That I was advocating this as a good thing! And that I believed that we would all, collectively as a society, quickly adopt the new technology to do online banking. And I was saying no such thing!

The problem? This gentleman heard what he wanted to hear. He was convinced that I was yet another technology prophet, predicting doom and gloom as the result of the computer age. He didn't hear me talk about how we can use this new capability to make better financial decisions; he saw me as someone who was saying that banks would soon disappear.

This is not a new problem, of course. All of our negative experiences with technology have engendered in our generation a cynicism towards things that are new. But we should keep in mind that there will also be those who predict doom and gloom with the arrival of any new technology and who raise alarmist warnings about what will happen. These doomsayers have been around for centuries.

> **In a recent address delivered at Columbia University, Mr. Edward W. Townsend, newspaper and magazine writer and Congressman, expressed the opinion that it was a misfortune that the typewriter had come to be so generally used in newspaper rooms, because it made the translation of thought into copy somewhat too easy. The view point is that the somewhat slower and more careful handwriting of any article or news item is better, clearer thought and is always better constructed when written with a fountain pen than when rambled off on a typewriter...**
>
> "Reporters Should Cultivate the Use of the Fountain Pen," *Pen Prophet*, the company publication of the Waterman pen company, Vol. XII, No. 1, June, 1914

Consider the Waterman pen company. In the early 1900s, new manufacturing techniques allowed the rapid adoption of typewriters in the world of business and the media. Some people expressed the belief that this was essentially a bad thing. Others bemoaned the thought that use of such a mechanical device would lead to the degradation in the quality of writing. We simply thought better when using a pen!

Such foolishness, you might think. But look around you today and observe what is being said about the computer age. You can find many people who loudly propound that the arrival of the word processor is a terribly bad thing and that the quality of writing is going to suffer. The saying that comes to mind for me is this: "what goes around, comes around." It seems that as a society we are doomed to repeat the negative predictions of yesterday.

Before the fountain pen, the arrival of the book was a bad thing! When Gutenberg invented the printing press, there was great concern that if the world were to provide the ability for anyone to publish, there would be a flood of lousy information. Said Jon Palfreman and Doron Swade, in their book *The Dream Machine — Exploring the Computer Age* (BBC Books, London, 1991), "What is true is that many of the same misconceptions about computers were held about books. Books are so ingrained in our culture that it is strange to think that they were once viewed as sacred objects."

Today, pundits argue that the Internet, which lets anyone publish electronically on a global basis, is a bad thing, since anyone can publish. Here we go again....

> **Said Thoth to the King of Egypt, "This invention, O King, will make the Egyptians wiser and will improve their memories; for it is an elixir of memory and wisdom that I have discovered," but the king was not convinced and feared that the invention of writing would impair the memory instead of improving it and that the people would read without understanding. (Plato)**
>
> *The Future of English, The Risks Digest,* Vol. 4, Issue 10, from the Internet

And when paper was invented, long before the age of technology, some predicted that it was not wise. Plato himself reported of a ruler who thought the invention of paper was a development that would cause people to lose their ability to think.

You get my point: our arrival into the information age of today is automatically met by many who are all too eager to counsel us on its potential for negativity.

With the introduction of anything new, especially the technologies of the information age, and the enormous ramifications of this new era, there will always be those who harp on the negative aspects, not acknowledging the potential benefits.

Perhaps they are scared; it is fair to say that we all fear the implications of technology, because it is something that is beyond our control. But that is no reason to close our minds to the possibilities that it presents or to focus solely on the negative implications.

Today, as with yesterday, the clarion call for some is that the computer is about to lead to massive layoffs; the information age is a development that will result in widespread unemployment, they cry, and we had best beware! There is some truth to this as we will see. The information age is leading to massive changes in jobs and careers, but millions of new jobs are created at the same time as old ones disappear.

We've seen such predictions of massive unemployment before, of course. At the same time that we saw rosy predictions made in the 1960s of the two- or three-day work week, there were others who predicted that its impact on jobs would be dreadful. They warned in dark and terrifying terms that the arrival of the computer would soon mean massive, disruptive change to our business world and that robots would be rampant, doing the work that man should be responsible for. Massive unemployment, far beyond our current rates of 10%, would be the result.

> In 1653 Blaise Pascal "introduced a working mechanical calculator. The Pascaline caused a sensation on the Continent (this despite the fact that it could only add and subtract), but Blaise was unable to find buyers for his wondrous machine. People said it was too complicated to operate, sometimes made mistakes and could be repaired only by its inventor. They also feared it would take jobs away from bookkeepers and other clerks."
>
> Marguerite Zientara, "History's Great Computer Eccentrics," in *Digital Deli*, edited by Steven Ditlea (Workman Publishing Company, New York, 1984)

Of course, such thinking wasn't new; in fact, it has been with us for as long as there has been progress with technology. Back in 1653, for example, the career potential for bookkeepers was up in the air, as one of the true forefathers of the computer age, Blaise Pascal, developed an early mechanical calculator. I marvel at this, given my training and successful career as a Chartered Accountant.

What has gone wrong here? The focus on negativity and the fact that throughout history we have failed to learn from the potential inaccuracy of alarmist predictions concerning unemployment, jobs and careers. Perhaps it is the unique nature of humans to focus on bad things, before the good things. One need only watch the evening news to appreciate this.

When the computer arrived on the scene, it was almost the perfect technology to allow for such alarmist predictions. And predictions there were: the U.S. Bureau of Labor Statistics estimated that 300,000 workers were being replaced annually by machines during the 1960s, and the American Foundation of Employment and Automation calculated that 2 million jobs a year were disappearing!

In the article "Why Work?" in *Newsweek*, February 12, 1962, it was noted that "in the next twenty years...the United States will be pushed...towards a very scary reliance on the machine. And unless American society prepares for it, says [Donald A.] Michael, there will be such chaotic disruption, loss of human values, and mass unemployment that the Great Depression will look like history's honeymoon by comparison. In his somber projection, prepared for the Fund for the Republic's Center for the Study of Democratic Institutions, Michael predicts that 'in twenty years, most of the routine blue-collar and white-collar tasks that can be done by cybernation will be.'" Other similar reports appeared with frequency: in May, 1964, the same publication carried an article predicting that up to 40,000 jobs were disappearing *every week* because of the computer. At this rate, in excess of 68 million jobs should have disappeared by now.

Today? Even as I wrote this chapter, I came across a headline in *The Globe and Mail*: "Unskilled Lose Jobs To Computers." I hear individuals on the radio and see them interviewed on TV, crying out that the wired world, the information age, is going to have a dramatic, dastardly effect. But my newspaper that tells me that even though we have stagnant unemployment of around 10%, millions of jobs have been created through the last decade. I mostly turn off my mind to most people who raise such alarming predictions, for I think that generally they don't really have a clue of what they are talking about.

What really happens is this: any new technology doesn't necessarily replace or lead to the destruction of something else. Whether that be jobs or something else. With the Internet today, some predict that it will replace television, books and newspapers. I doubt that will happen.

After all, when television came along, many predicted that it would replace radio. Today, of course, the radio industry is strong, booming and in no imminent danger of collapse. And when radio came along, there were those who predicted that the ability to pick up music through the air would have a disastrous effect on the business of manufacturing pianos and other musical instruments. Talking movies created many new jobs, but put many musicians out of work. The cycle goes on and on, with

> **Imagination is the key to motivation.**
>
> Rene Descartes

the end result that many new technologies do not replace other things, but supplement them.

The change in our economic systems is ongoing: in 1930, 30 million farmers produced for 100 million people, while today, roughly 3 million farmers produce food for 250 million people. Why? Technology has played a major role. What happened to the rest of the farmers? The trend to urbanization has led to a society in which those who might have been farmers simply do other things.

Examples abound of specific jobs that have disappeared. In 1980 there were 300,000 people employed in manufacturing and maintaining automobile carburetors. The introduction of electronic fuel injection equipment eliminated those jobs within five years. Is the automobile industry as a whole dead? No, of course not. Is it very different than it was in 1980, with new jobs appearing as old ones disappear? Yes.

So it is with the things we take for granted in our day-to-day lives. Online banking won't come to replace our visits to the bank; it will for many people simply be another convenient alternative, one that they might use little or much of the time.

The fellow who called me on the radio station? I feel sorry for the fact that his blindness to what is truly occurring will rob him of opportunity.

> **If we are to learn anything from the history of computers...it ought to be extreme care in predicting what computers will mean to the society and the culture.**
> Fred Hapgood, "Computers Aren't So Smart After All," *Atlantic Monthly*, August, 1974

What gets me is the negativity that surrounds this new age that we are entering. How can you expect and even hope to survive, if your only attitude is that all of this change is a bad thing? How can you close your mind and hope to have a chance of living through the change, if you are convinced that everything that is happening will lead to negative situations. How can you be a survivor, if you listen and believe the pundits with their cries of doom, at the same time being aware that they all too often repeat the failed predictions of the past?

My advice? Be one of those who sees the glass as half full. Make a deliberate effort to find the good aspects first. They may be hard to find sometimes, but putting yourself on the positive side of the technology will help take some of the scariness out of it.

Another reason for a positive outlook? If you are a parent, think about your children. Do you want to instill in them a negative attitude with respect to the world in which they will grow up? I think not. Hence you should, as a parent, ensure that you pass on a positive attitude about the information age to your children.

18

Accepting the Inevitability of Change

> *It is hard to let old beliefs go. They are familiar. We are comfortable with them and have spent years building systems and developing habits that depend on them. Like a man who has worn eyeglasses so long that he forgets he has them on, we forget that the world looks to us the way it does because we have become used to seeing it that way through a particular set of lenses. Today, however, we need new lenses. And we need to throw the old ones away.*
>
> Kenich Ohmae

Whether it is in our business or personal lives, change is inevitable. Some changes are easier to deal with than others, but we all begin each new day, discovering that something is different. The changes that are self-initiated are easy to deal with; after all, we are responsible for those particular changes. But the type of change involving events that are out of our control is often the most difficult to deal with.

The arrival of the information age fits into this second category. It is a sweeping tide of change that is clearly beyond our capability to control. How do you react? Some have tried to cope by fighting back, with limited success. In fact, history bears witness to the stories of those, who, rather than trying to accept and deal with the change that is occurring, try to deny what is happening or choose to fight against it.

> **Inside yourself or outside, you never have to change what you see, only the way you see it.**
>
> Thaddeus Golas

For instance, in 1969, Harvey Matusow founded the International Society for the Abolition of Data Processing Machines, which he claimed boasted a membership of some 1,500 people. The group looked upon "the computer as an exploitive monster that has turned on its creator," according to the article "Guerrilla War Against Computers," printed in *Time* magazine, September 12, 1969.

Matusow and his group were convinced that computers were evil machines and that mankind should not only resist but fight against their coming dominance in our day-to-day lives. Matusow himself suggested a number of approaches, such as:

• not simply folding, spindling or mutilating punch cards, but carefully "reprogramming" them by cutting additional tiny holes in them to confuse the electronic brains;

• erasing the magnetic coding on personal cheques so that each cheque would have to be handled by a human, so that it would "get the loving care it deserves";

• destroying the return portion of a computerized bill and sending the payment with a handwritten note instead, indicating why;

• pasting stamps on sideways so that computerized sorters could not read them.

There were all kinds of other actions, all with the intent of somehow turning back the course of change sweeping the world of business at the time. Such actions seem quaint and even humorous today, but, clearly, Matusow failed in his mission. I wonder what he is doing today.

There are many who deal with technological change well and therefore "get it." But there are many more who "do not get it" and try to force their negative views about the information age on others. There are still many people like Harvey Matusow around today, the Lead Pencil Society, for example, who proudly identify themselves as "Luddites," intent on resisting technology. I find that people like Matusow tend to exert a form of peer pressure on others. For some, it has become "trendy" to slam the opportunities for personal opportunity to be found by mastering the information age.

> **It is hard enough to alter your mental attitude without people encouraging you to avoid change, particularly the change that is occurring with the information age. If we don't change direction soon, we'll end up where we're going.**
>
> Professor Irwin Corey

Dealing with change can be difficult. At some point most of us have probably wished for the world to slow down; after all, continuous and ongoing change is often all too difficult to deal with. But we also know that the world won't slow down, that change is inevitable.

How do we deal with the relentless change occurring around us? Perhaps one way is by recognizing that the rate of change is accelerating rather than slowing, particularly in the area of computer technology. Forcing ourselves to accept this will help put us into a mindset in which we can accept such change, because we know it will be continuous and never-ending.

Consider this: some researchers think that 80% of the technology that we might use 10 or 20 years from now has yet to be invented. Now consider the implications of such a statement: at least half of the "stuff" that you might be using in your home, office and your life in the near future may not even exist yet in the minds of those who will invent it. Who knows what riches — and struggles — we are in for?

If there were ever a clarion call for the inevitably of change, it has to be recognition that no one has even dreamed up many of the new things that will enter our lives over the next decade.

And through the next decades, computer and telecommunications technology will likely evolve at a faster rate than any other technology. The potential implications will be even more dramatic than they have been over the last 30 years.

How fast? No one is certain; even the experts can't agree. Gordon Bell, who is generally acknowledged as the inventor of the transistor, estimates that the computer hardware of 2002 will be 1,000 times more powerful than that of 1987. Some of his counterparts disagree; they think that it will be about 1 million times more powerful. That's a pretty big difference. But is it? Does the magnitude of difference matter to us? Not really; all we can be certain of is that these machines will become faster, more powerful and capable of even more interesting things.

The changes in telecommunications capabilities will be even more dramatic than the changes in computer technology.

When I grew up, the *Encyclopedia Britannica* was a trusted and willing friend; many a school project depended upon my ability to ferret out nuggets of information from within its pages. My parents went so far as to buy an entire set in 1964, a significant purchase for them at the time. It was well used by all eight kids in our family.

A few years ago, I came across an article reporting that scientists were working on telecommunications technology for the future that would permit blazingly fast transmission speeds. How fast? They suggested that it would be possible to transmit the entire *Encyclopedia Britannica* from coast to coast in less than a second.

I don't know about you, but that boggles my mind! Looking back at the articles from the 1950s and 1960s that I researched for this book, I see that, while many predictions were far-fetched and never came true, many others did come true.

I happen to believe this one. Like many, I think we are on the cusp of development of many new technologies that will permit the exchange and distribution of absolutely massive volumes of information worldwide. To me, the world is becoming wired, and I don't think any of us fully appreciate how big a change that will bring. We can see only a tantalizing glimpse of it today.

Certainly, there is no doubt that we will see new computers that are going to be faster, smaller and less expensive. They will continue to invade other aspects of our lives, whether that be the homes in which we sleep or the offices in which we work. Stereos, televisions, radios, appliances — anything and everything will continue to become computerized to a degree that we cannot even begin to imagine.

How quickly things might move forward is anyone's guess, and it should come as no surprise that there are mixed messages on what we might see. I should have convinced you by now that outcomes in the future are truly unpredictable.

Coping with change also means you must deal with the rate at which that change occurs. You must get used to a life that will be constantly and suddenly changing, going out-of-date or becoming obsolete. No doubt the computers we use today will provoke snickers ten years from now, if not

Today is the tomorrow you worried about yesterday.
Unknown

sooner. So we must be prepared to live in a world of instant obsolescence.

The pace of change is speeding up, not slowing down. Other generations have not had to deal with such a rapid pace of change. In the book *The Future — Trends and Developments Through the 21st Century* (a Lyle Stuart book, published by Carol Publishing Group, New Jersey, 1990), author Ronald D. Rotstein noted that "people living in the sixteenth or seventeenth century were secure in the knowledge that the way they lived, the horse-drawn carriages that conveyed them, the tools they used, and the food they consumed were more or less the same as what their grandparents had had and their grandchildren would have.... Then came the Industrial Revolution. With the steam engine and then a deluge of inventions tapping other sources of energy, such as electricity, the pace of change quickened. Yet even into the first half of the twentieth century the rate of change was manageable. The future still remained on the horizon. The Wright Brothers took man aloft and that was wondrous; still. Progress in flight and aircraft was spread over decades....Mankind had time to adjust. Even manned flight to the moon was a ten-year adventure. It took time for the telephone to spread from Alexander Graham Bell's lab to almost every household in America. It took decades for television, which was invented in the twenties, to broadcast Milton Berle hamming it up for millions of people. Today that grace period for adjustment to development is disappearing. The distance between now and the future has been shortened dramatically by advanced telecommunications and computers.... Information flows in minutes where once it took days or weeks."

We can see this in our daily lives. For example, it took a good 10 or 15 years for a broad cross section of society to come to accept the use of automatic banking machines. But the period of acceptance for debit cards was much shorter: two or three years. And now, trials of new electronic cash cards seem to compress the acceptance time even further; it seems these trials already indicate sectors of the population ready and willing to use them.

> **Typewriters, 8-track audio players, vinyl records, and a host of other products and services disappeared in roughly a five-year period due to new technology. A five-year period of change is now common.**
>
> "Technology and wealth," *Journal of the American Society of CLU & ChFC*, January, 1996

Looking around my home, I can see signs of the graveyard of change. My collection of LP records, which I will likely never use again, remains; it is too hard to throw these relics away. My CD-ROM collection grows, and I am told that one day, these too will be obsolete as I obtain the ability to instantly access music from any other computer on the planet.

Three old personal computers have sat far away in a basement crawl space for years. Ten years or older, and so obviously out-of-date that they are useless, but I've convinced myself they might be worthy of something one day.

I have some 8-mm movies, although I don't have a projector. I am told that my VCR will soon be replaced by a new technology known as recordable digital video disc. On and on it goes. The technology in my life tends to be fleeting, visiting me for a short period of time, only to disappear when it is replaced by something else.

We struggle with this reality, but I don't think that our kids do. So I think part of our difficulty in accepting change is because never before have we had a technology generation gap such as this one.

Going back in time, we can see that parents and children usually experienced the same technology; it didn't change that much in a lifetime. But today it is very different. Our kids have come to accept — even expect — that change is constant and never-ending. Constantly clamouring for the latest video game release or hot new personal entertainment toy, they are growing up in a world in which they have come to expect the inevitability of rapid and dramatic change. Yet we hold on to the old ways, uncomfortable and never totally accepting of a world in which change is measured in days and months rather than years and decades.

If you are to survive the information age, you must be willing to accept the inevitable and dramatic change that will come with it. To get into the right frame of mind of accepting change, here are some things you should do:

1. Try to avoid people who try to deny the changes that are occurring, because they will only make it more difficult to alter your attitude. Resist the peer pressure trying to encourage you to be negative to what is occurring; adopt a positive outlook!

2. To be a survivor means you need to accept the inevitability of the change that the information age will bring about. Accept that tomorrow's world will be very different from today and prepare yourself to be swept along with the tide.

19

What Does It Mean to Live in the Information Age?

> *...as technology helps its possessors acquire ever-greater amounts of knowledge, the pace keeps accelerating. According to information-technology analyst Peter Keen, as much new text is now published each day as all of civilization produced from the invention of writing to the beginning of the nineteenth century.*
>
> Arno Penzias, *Harmony — Business, Technology & Life After Paperwork*
> (Harper Business, New York, 1995)

How the heck do we ensure our survival in the age of information if we aren't quite sure exactly what is expected of us in the information age? This is not a hypothetical question; I find that many people are confused and simply don't understand what they have to do to be a winner.

This is a unique state of affairs. After all, it was easy for people living in the agricultural age to understand what was expected of them. More than likely, their survival came from their ability to work the land and maximize the harvest, as society began to develop the ability for food production on a scale not previously seen. And the role of someone in the industrial age was easy to understand; success in those types of jobs was likely dependent upon the ability to deal with the new technology emerging in the industrial world, as society came to place increasing reliance on large-scale production methods fueled by technological progress.

In both cases success came to those with the ability to master the technology of the era, whether it was a plow or a cotton gin.

> **The illiterate of the 21st century will not be those who cannot read and write, but those who cannot learn, unlearn and relearn.**
>
> Alvin Toffler

So it is with the information age: success will come to those who can master the fundamental technology of the age as found with the computer. But it's not just that. An important survival skill in the information age will be to deal with volumes of information on a scale not previously available to mankind.

The computer is the foundry of the information age, an invention that is responsible for fueling a worldwide explosion of information. Give someone a computer, and you are giving him his own printing press.

It is a device that is truly unparalleled in terms of its ability to generate information. And if you link the capability of the computer to generate information to the approaching revolution in telecommunications technologies, which permits the linking of millions of computers worldwide, then we all will soon have the capability to publish our thoughts and knowledge for a worldwide audience.

The result? Massive increases in the availability of information. Current estimates by people who study such things are that every four or five years, the total amount of available information doubles.

Imagine if every four or five years, the number of books and magazines carried in your local library were to double. Imagine seeing all the trucks containing the most recent shipment of titles lined up at the library loading dock, as libraries try to cope with the influx of new material. And imagine the stress of the librarians simply trying to catalogue all of these new books!

> **I am entirely certain that twenty years from now we will look back at education as it is practiced in most schools today and wonder that we could have tolerated anything so primitive.**
>
> John W. Gardner

The effects are rather extreme in the longer term. Some predict that, given current rates of growth, the total of all human knowledge that was available in 1993 will be but 1% of what will be available to our children in 2050. In other words, take each library in your community and multiply the size of each by 100!

The early signs of such growth rates in information availability are already here, and the bad news is that too much information is a problem, not a solution. Many scientists and researchers feel that even in this early stage of the information age, they are beginning to suffer from information overload. Anyone working in a field that involves some type of specialty research, whether medical, scientific or theoretical in nature, is suffering from this overload of information; there are too many research papers, documents, reports, news articles and other volumes of information. Many people are complaining that they simply cannot keep up! We are drowning in a flood of information and will soon be deluged.

And from my perspective, survival will come to those who can deal with such massive quantities of information and, more importantly, from the ability to transform information into knowledge. After all, you can have all the information in the world, but without the ability to analyze and learn from it, information by itself is useless.

I look around my home office and realize that I've taken some positive steps towards achieving that goal. Years ago, I purposefully set out to try to master the skill of "turning information into knowledge." I've done several things that have convinced me that I've managed to turn myself into a true "knowledge worker."

For example, I have learned to reuse and recycle much of the information that I have generated and have come across over the last ten years. For more than a decade, much of my day-to-day business activities have been characterized by the use of electronic mail and by the documents that I type into my word processing software. Regardless of what book or client project I might be working on, I regularly use my computer to send and receive all kinds of e-mail messages during a normal day, and have been doing so for almost 15 years. And I type most of my own reports and letters.

> **Education's purpose is to replace an empty mind with an open one.**
>
> Malcolm S. Forbes

Much of what goes back and forth through my electronic mailbox involves little things: arrangements for meetings, thank you messages and many letters and documents that I have typed that have little lasting value. But scattered throughout all the messages and documents, there is some information that is useful.

Way back in 1984, I decided that it was important to keep most of my e-mail and documents, regardless of how useless such information might be. So I have now amassed some pretty large computer files containing hundreds of thousands of messages, documents, reports, letters and other information.

This has become an invaluable knowledge tool. If am working on a book, a news or magazine article, a client seminar or a consulting project, I can be pretty certain that buried in all of that information is a nugget directly relevant to what I am doing. I use several programs to help me locate specific pieces of information buried within those files, turning them into an invaluable resource!

I've taught myself to recycle my own information and to extract knowledge from my own electronic database, and that, I think, is a good skill to have in the information age.

Of course, all of this might be rather meaningless to you. After all, a lot of the information generated by the information age itself is simply hype and hyperbole. Scan the business press and you can come across statements such as "97% of all employment growth is coming from 'knowledge work'" and that "by 1995, trade in knowledge industries has become 25% of total trade." What is "knowledge work," and what is a "knowledge industry"?

How do you take such grandiose statements and put them into a real, practical perspective, such as "what must I do to keep my job and keep earning an income through the next few decades?"

One way to do this is by understanding that the fundamentals of many basic jobs are changing, such that performance of the job is itself becoming "knowledge-intensive." This means that the ability to perform that job will come to depend on one's ability to master the technology that comes with the job. It will also come from the ability to master the increasing volumes of information that are related by the performance of the job. And we are already seeing various jobs around the world that are becoming information-dependent.

Take a simple farmer. Thirty years ago, success might have come from the ability to keep the field tilled, the livestock fed and cared for and the tractor in a state of good repair. But even farming has gone high-tech. Intelligent devices are entering the farming industry, turning the average farmer into a farm manager overseeing smart farms. The ability to keep on top of global weather trends, world-wide commodity prices, the latest in genetic engineering research and scientific advances in livestock management and yield is becoming as critical to the success of the farm as good dirt. Many farmers live in the wired world; before heading out into the field in their tractors, they often first check information sources from the wired world that could affect what they might do that day.

Consider police officers; the image of an officer walking a beat is already out-of-date. Most major police forces in the country already feature computer-equipped cars, such that the average officer is well armed with information. In the future, the potential of efforts to nab the "bad guy" will not come solely from good police investigative work, but from skills in ferreting out useful information from global crime databases and other information sources that might lead them to the culprit.

> **Change does not necessarily assure progress, but progress implacably requires change. Education is essential to change, for education creates both new wants and the ability to satisfy them.**
>
> Henry Steele Commager

The traveling salesman is wired. Many sell their wares and services from fully equipped mobile offices and vans. From the front seats of their cars they can access the combined knowledge, talent and expertise of the distributors, manufacturers and other companies that they represent. Their survival increasingly comes from a willingness to use the tools of the information age to determine how they can best accomplish their goal in life: to sell stuff! Knowledge skills involve determining how to mine the information sources at their disposal, ranging from corporate sales statistics and other information to keeping on top of local and global trends and developments that might affect their customers. If they can turn all of this information into knowledge that can help them land the deal, they are a success.

Aircraft pilots are less the daring and dashing masters of the cockpit than they are supervisors of flight equipment and masters of various information sources. Travel on a sophisticated jet such as an Airbus 320, and you are taking a voyage on a plane that mostly flies itself. It can even land on its own! During a flight, the pilot does less flying and more interacting with a myriad of computers feeding him or her information, everything from the status of the equipment, the progress of the flight and in-transit and destination weather conditions to news updates from a computer back at corporate head office concerning fuel usage and efficiency. Their success in the job comes less from basic flying than it comes from mastering information.

Individual factory workers are going hi-tech. Robots are real and are found in many factories, although they bear little resemblance to the mechanical humanoids of science fiction. And an ever-increasing number of assembly-line jobs, once the basis of routine, mechanical steps performed over and over, are being replaced by various technological devices that allow the factory worker to monitor information, everything concerning the progress of the line, the specifics of a particular assembly or production records and plans.

No matter where you turn, the reality of the information age is that it is coming to mean that the ability to deal with ever-increasing amounts of information on a day-to-day basis in the performance of a job is becoming paramount.

But there are other important skills beyond dealing with lots of information, such as the ability to obtain knowledge from that information, often on very short notice. Through the last decade, I've spent a lot of time teaching myself how to do electronic research, developing the ability to harvest knowledge from information. If a client calls me with a question about a particular topic or issue, I will often go off and undertake a search of several electronic databases that publish the words of tens of thousands of magazines and newspapers, since that is often a good source of background information. If I need to know the corporate history of a particular organization or need to know a little about someone with whom I might meet, I'll see what background I can discover in the wired world.

What have I taught myself to do? I've learned to get information just when I need it! Ask me about some hot new management trend, and in 24 hours I'll have made myself an expert on the topic by harnessing research and news reports from around the world.

Not only do I go out and obtain knowledge when I need it; I've taught myself to track particular topics and issues so that I can keep my knowledge about the topic in a finely tuned state. I use the tools of the information age, such as they are today, to run a sophisticated system on my computer that in effect goes out and scans the globe for information that might be relevant to what I do or might be important to a particular project that I am working on.

In effect, I am teaching myself to master the capabilities of the computer; only the information that I need and might be relevant to me need enter my domain.

The result of these skills? To some, I look like I am pretty knowledgeable about certain issues and appear to be an expert on a broad range of other issues. But what I have really done is quite unique; I've become a master of the ability to turn information into knowledge. In short, my computer is my information tool; it serves me, not the other way around.

I like to say that by doing all of this, I have learned to obtain "just-in-time" knowledge. This is a critical and important survival skill and perhaps the most important skill for surviving in the information age.

What does this mean? You will be buffeted by the forces of the information age in the next 5 to 20 years, a key result of which is a heck of a lot of information. Turning this information into knowledge will be one of the key ways of ensuring your survival.

What should you do? Any number of things:

The more you use your brain, the more brain you will have to use.

George A Dorsey

1. I'm convinced that being able to do electronic research is an important and useful skill. Learn how to find information on the Internet and using the CD-ROM encyclopedias at your

local library. Discover what you can do to use tools that electronically track news topics of relevance to you. Whatever you do, discover the magic of information in the information age.

2. Start building your own library of information. Anything that you have in electronic form is a valuable asset. Keep it! It might seem irrelevant to you today, but who knows how it might be useful to you ten years from now!

3. Take a look at your job or career, and ask yourself how it might change through the next decade. Take a look at industry newsletters and publications and see what they have to say about the changes forthcoming to your own industry or profession. Spend some time, in effect, discovering how your job might be transformed into a knowledge career in the future. Once you have a good idea of that reality, then start doing what is necessary to master those skills.

As we shall see, the corporate world will soon come to rely on those who can cope in a new workplace in which the sharing of knowledge and information is the key cultural trait of the company. Becoming a "knowledge worker" is all about learning how to transform massive volumes of information into knowledge with the understanding that the old phrase "knowledge is power" is truly becoming relevant.

20

The Wired World of Business

> *...technology does not avalanche overnight into the mainstream of daily life; it takes time, and there are all kinds of fights and rear-guard actions as individuals and organizations try to avoid the pain and discomfort of change.*
>
> "The revolution in the workplace: What's happening to our jobs?"
> *The Futurist,* March/April, 1996

We are at a crossroads in the way that the world of business uses computer technology. Through the next decade, large portions of the global economy are going to move into the wired world, as the transactions that drive business today, many of which are still paper-based, go electronic. This will come about as the business world invests an incredible amount of time and effort in extending the reach of their computer systems to other systems outside of the organization. To date, many of these systems have been used for internal purposes only. These changes are expected to have an impact on every type of business. This in itself should be encouragement enough for you to be a participant in the information age.

To understand what is going to happen, you don't need a lot of fancy new-age management buzzwords and business gurus to guide you. You simply need to understand how computers have been used to this point in the business world and how they will be used in the future.

The facts are simply this: companies and organizations have essentially spent the last 20 or 30 years figuring out how to computerize their own operations, and they have largely succeeded in doing so. Today, sophisticated electronic mail systems, databases, production, control and financial systems allow an organization to manage information internally on a company-wide basis. The corporate world has been transformed as a result.

But the corporate world is still truly an infant when it comes to computerization. While most companies have learned how to use computers to support their internal activities, few have linked their computer systems to those of their customers, suppliers, trading partners and business associates.

Nothing great was ever achieved without enthusiasm.

R.W. Emerson

You can certainly understand this in terms of the computer that you might use at work. Most likely, you can use it to reach other people within the company, and you can probably access a few corporate information resources, financial systems or other internal information. But if you are like most people, the reach of your computer doesn't extend to companies outside of your own; at best, you might be able to send electronic mail to anyone around the world or access Web sites. The way you interact with other companies is probably using phone calls, meetings, faxes and through the exchange of invoices, purchase orders, requisitions and other forms of paper documentation.

Now suppose your company links its financial and other computer systems to those companies with whom it does business, so that you can interact electronically with them, no matter where they might be in the world. Suddenly, what you do on a day-to-day basis begins to change.

The article "An American renaissance in the year 2000: 74 trends that will affect America's future — And yours," in *The Futurist* in March/April, 1994 gave a good overview of what is going on: "New industrial standards—for building materials, fasteners, even factory machinery—allow both civilian and government buyers to order from any supplier, rather than only from those with whom they have established relationships....To aid "just-in-time" purchasing, many suppliers are giving customers direct, on-line access to their computerized ordering and inventory systems. The order may go directly from the customer to the shop floor, and even into the supplier's automated production equipment. Many manufacturers will no longer deal with suppliers who cannot provide this access."

Your ability to cope in that new wired business world, one that involves a global economy that is increasingly computerized, will have a direct impact on your career and job success.

Fifteen years back, while working with the public accounting firm where I received my training as a Chartered Accountant, I undertook the audit of many organizations of all sizes. I also provided taxation, business advisory and consulting services to these organizations. It was invaluable training; I got to see a lot of what made companies "tick."

Whenever we started a new audit, several of us would effectively camp out at one of our clients, with the objective of going through their financial systems with a fine-tooth comb. It was our task to become intimately familiar with their financial systems — the methods in which they billed their customers and received and processed payments and cheques and the procedures they undertook to pay suppliers. The financial systems we dealt with were sometimes computerized, and often not.

> **Sir Leon Bagrit, a British cyberneticist, was quoted as saying, "The pace of technical change is so fast now that we must be**

> **prepared for a man to change not only his job, but his entire skills, three or four times in a lifetime."**
> "The revolution in the workplace: What's happening to our jobs?"
> *The Futurist*, March/April, 1996

As part of our job, we would interview the people who were the lifeblood of many of these companies: payroll, accounts payable and accounts receivable clerks, corporate comptrollers, accounting managers, shipping dock staff and inventory managers. In essence, by talking with these people, we learned all about how information flowed through the organization.

In more than one situation, computers were being introduced into the workplace while we were there, and I had the opportunity to watch firsthand how these people reacted. And even back then, I noticed that many people my age and older were simply terrified as the first wave of computerization entered the company.

> **...the really beneficial impacts of a new technology don't arise until two-thirds of the way through the transition ... that moment is just ahead, in the next five to 10 years. The new integrated information technology, highly refined and matured, is about to avalanche into all of our homes and workplaces, enriching and complicating daily life for everybody.**
> "The revolution in the workplace: What's happening to our jobs?"
> *The Futurist*, March/April, 1996

Some did not react well to the changes. I remember one lady in particular, a clerk in the accounts receivable department. She had been at the job for some 25 years and had been accustomed to working in a certain way. The impact of computerization meant that her day-to-day job — the processing of invoices — would change dramatically. She did not take well to the fact that someone was asking her to do her job in a different way, with a computer being involved at that! The result? She fought back as hard as she could, to the great frustration of management. She simply could not adapt; in effect, she could not accept the technology. I understand that she was eventually let go. She was a barrier to computerization. I often wonder what she is doing today and if she realizes the folly of her ways.

There are many people like her. I often think about many of my old clients today and wonder about the people who work for them. What is going to happen to them as this next wave of computerization sweeps their world, one that will see business organizations learning to do business with each other electronically? Will you be a casualty?

I think that we are in for some pretty significant changes in the way the business world works as a result of this next, new wave of computerization.

> By using high-speed data communications networks to track production, stock, and orders, GE Lighting has closed 26 of 34 U.S. warehouses since 1987 and replaced 25 customer service centers with one new, high-tech center. In effect, those buildings and stockpiles—physical assets—have been replaced by networks and databases—intellectual assets.
> Thomas A. Stewart, "Welcome to the revolution," *FORTUNE*, December 13, 1993

Think about what is going to happen. Instead of receiving orders by fax and telephone, customers will link to the computer of a supplier through the Internet in order to place orders directly. Payments will flow directly between companies in the form of electronic cash, eliminating or completely changing some of the cheque-processing systems that are in use today. Suppliers will make available and distribute electronic catalogues, rather than the cumbersome paper documents of today. Invoices will be paid electronically with a few strokes on a keyboard, rather than by preparing and printing cheques. Employee benefit claims will be made directly to a third-party insurance company through an online form, rather than through a cumbersome paper form. There will be a gradual and steady reduction in the exchange of paper between organizations, as the business world discovers what it takes to conduct what many refer to as electronic commerce.

We've seen the signs of such change in companies that have already leapt into this new electronic world. Airlines, the auto industry, the retail industry and some manufacturing sectors have seen significant changes in the way they work — and in their workforce — as a result of interorganization computerization.

What will happen to people who work within the corporate world through the next decade as other industries are impacted by such change?

Sadly, I know that there will be many who will resist, fight back and belittle such efforts. They will be unwilling to accept what is happening and will do their best not to take part. They will be like the accounts receivable clerk I watched years ago. And management, forced by the competitive realities of the emerging wired world, will have no choice but to let them go.

Then there will be others who will be willing to accept the change, work with it and help to make it a success. These will be the survivors.

Companies will start all kinds of projects to move to this new wave of computerization; many are already underway.

As you deal with such projects and efforts as they inevitably begin to occur around you, it's important that you keep an open mind! You should also seek out personal opportunity within these projects with the clear objective of determining how you can advance (or keep) your own position within the company.

As you do so, it's important that you throw out any "baggage" that you might have from past projects. Many people who went through computer upgrades and large-scale systems projects in the last decade in the companies in which they worked often had a lot of bad experiences. Getting computerized was not something that sped things up; it seemed to slow things down! Such projects were not smooth and straightforward, and there is nothing to say that this new wave of computerization will be. Mistakes will occur, difficulties will be encountered and it will be a slow and painful process.

The difficulty of implementation of such projects is made all the worse through the fact that many people will resist such change. Your survival will come from the ability to get involved in such projects, to support them, encourage them and help to make them work!

Think about the type of person you want to be with this new era of computerization. You don't want to end up being one of those people who young people dread having to deal with at work because you refuse to open your mind to future possibilities. Refuse to be an information age curmudgeon! As these projects come about, embrace them!

> **I do not fear computers.**
>
> **I fear the lack of them.**
>
> Issac Asimov

How do you do this? Think back to your early work days, the early stage of your career. Was there someone whom you avoided because he refused to listen to new ideas? Did you often get frustrated with the "powers-that-be" because they often seemed to have closed minds to new initiatives that made sense? Did you suffer from anger because top management just didn't seem to understand your own ideas? Is there still a lot of coffee-hour chatter about office politics and how "so-and-so" just can't seem to change?

And now ask yourself: are you becoming that type of person, because of the way that you deal with the changes that the information age is bringing to our corporate world? Don't let it happen to you!

Often, this means that you have to open up your mind to new ideas as they are presented. If you are in management, your survival can often come from a willingness to accept and encourage change within those who report to you. If an employee comes to you with a good idea, instead of just saying "write a report" or "send me a note," work with her to encourage her idea or sit with him and walk through his suggestions. Not only will you benefit in that you will have a better understanding of what the employee is suggesting, but you may learn a thing or two about how your systems work.

If you aren't in management, feel free to make suggestions to those who are! They will be struggling with the methods and procedures to introduce the new forms of computerization and will be open to ideas from those who are enthusiastic about the project. Open your mind to the possibilities of this new form of electronic business and be a player, rather than a viewer on the sidelines.

There is no doubt that there are both positive and negative implications to the way that our world of business will change in the years to come. A wired economy, as it takes hold, will cause untold havoc to the lives of many, at the same time that it provides opportunity to others. That is reality; the world in which we live often presents to us the good as it deals the bad.

Your goal is to survive, to ensure that you do not become a casualty. How do you do this? By being prepared:

> **They say that time changes things, but actually you have to change them yourself.**
>
> Andy Warhol

1. Study the industry in which you work once again, this time with a view to understanding how it might change in the emerging wired economy. What are companies on the leading edge doing? What types of information technology projects are underway, and why are these projects occurring? How is the industry being transformed as a result of the interlinking of computers between different companies?

2. Take a look at other industries that have already been affected: airlines, the retail industry and others come to mind. Study companies such as Wal-Mart, companies that have truly transformed the way they work by implementing sophisticated inventory and ordering systems.

3. Take some time to understand the technologies that will come to play in the wired economy, for example, the Internet and electronic data interchange; these are the tools of the new economy.

4. Get involved in projects at work! Volunteer! Become part of the team that is struggling to define the future direction and strategies of the company or simply get involved with the technology in any way you can.

5. Be prepared to learn! It doesn't hurt to study management magazines; publications like *Forbes*, *Business Week* and *Canadian Business* are full of stories about how companies are transforming themselves through external information technology links. Examine such articles, and think about how those types of transformations would affect you directly in your own job.

I'm convinced that this new era is going to be fascinating for many — and very dangerous for many others. But you must open your eyes up to the potential both ways, as it begins to occur.

21

The Knowledgeable Organization

...intellectual capital — knowledge that can be captured and deployed to create advantage over competitors — is as vital a business concern as capital of the familiar monetary sort.... In 1991, business investment in computers and telecommunications equipment — tools of the new economy that create, sort, store, and ship knowledge — for the first time exceeded capital spending for industrial, construction, and other "old economy" equipment.

Thomas A. Stewart, "Welcome to the revolution," FORTUNE, December 13, 1993

When GE built the parking lot for its appliance factory in Louisville, Kentucky, in 1953, it provided for 25,000 cars, but today, only 10,000 of those parking spaces are in use. In 1985, 406,000 people worked for IBM, a company that happily proclaimed that it had a no-layoff policy. Today? Perhaps but two-thirds of that number have full-time jobs. In 1995, AT&T announced the largest layoff in history: 77,000 managers were given notice on one single day.

> **According to a 1995 survey of 2,000 corporate executives from the world's leading industrial nations, 94 percent of the respondents reported that their companies had been through a reorganization in the past two years, resulting in a permanent reduction in their workforce. More than 66 percent of the business leaders predicted that the pace of downsizing and reengineering would increase in the years ahead.**
>
> Jeremy Rifkin, *The End of Work* (G.P. Putnam's Sons, New York, 1995)

Today, it is still not unusual to hear of a Fortune 1000 organization announcing layoffs involving numbers in the thousands, as the roll call of the corporate downsizing era continues. And we are deluding ourselves if we think that the era of employee rationalization is over, or if we think that our jobs are safe. For the business world is in the midst of discovering that the true magic of the information age is not only found in the ability to crunch a lot of numbers, as with the financial, inventory and production systems of today, but in that it permits employees to share information and knowledge in ways that have never been possible.

We've been able to poke a lot of fun in this book at predictions made about technology; we can giggle at the predicted robots and talking computers of the past that just have not come to be. But many management experts did predict that the impact of computers in the workforce would be felt most dramatically in the ranks of what we call "middle management" and that computers would soon lead to significant downsizing in the workplace.

In fact, there is a remarkably accurate track record from management gurus who predicted that an era of significant downsizing and corporate upheaval would soon be upon us as the result of the arrival of computer technology, as business organizations automated the process of crunching numbers. Indeed, as far back as 1958, certainly the earliest days of the computer revolution by any stretch of the imagination, there were some who foresaw that computers would have a dreadful impact, particularly on the role of middle management. That prediction most certainly came true and is one that continues today, as the corporate world continues to downsize with abandon.

> In 1958 *Harvard Business Review* published an article called "Management in the 1980s" by Harold J. Leavitt and Thomas L. Whisler, professors at the Carnegie Institute of Technology and the University of Chicago. It predicted that the computer would do to middle management what the Black Death did to 14th-century Europeans. So it has: If you're middle management and still have a job, don't enter your boss's office alone. Says GE Lighting's John Opie: "There are just two people between me and a salesman—information technology replaced the rest."
>
> Thomas A. Stewart, "Welcome to the revolution," *FORTUNE*, December 13, 1993

Why do computers cause people to lose their jobs? Because computers now process much of the information that was processed by people. Think about this: before computers came along, companies had to hire lots of staff whose sole responsibility was to manage information involving accounting, financial, production and other sorts of systems. The role of many employees was to summarize information into a short, concise and digestible form suitable for senior management.

The job of many employees was to process information and push paper, a responsibility that provided a suitable and long-lasting career for many, of course, until computers came along and took over that role of condensing information. As computers came to be implemented within organizations, businesses discovered that there was certainly less of a need for a lot of paper pushers. After all, why have paper pushers when you don't need to push paper any more?

The massive downsizing in executive ranks that has occurred, much of it through the last decade as companies finally figured out how to implement computer systems, is but the first massive downsizing era. New information technology capabilities that help organizations capture and share corporate knowledge will soon lead to the next one.

There are many challenges facing business today: globalization, or the necessity to operate and survive in a worldwide economy; increased competition — new companies can enter and compete in your market in a flash; automation, the world of electronic commerce, as we discussed in the previous chapter. Take a look around, and it's obvious that many business organizations struggle to survive on a day-to-day basis.

> **It's the survival of the fastest, not the fittest.**
> Alvin Toffler

In some ways, the impact of all of these pressures is that the world of business has had to learn to move very quickly. Organizations can no longer afford to take several weeks or months to make decisions; they must be lightning fast in their actions. As indicated in the article "Welcome to the revolution," by Thomas A. Stewart, in *FORTUNE*, December 13, 1993, "Management today has to think like a fighter pilot. When things move so fast, you can't always make the right decision—so you have to learn to adjust, to correct more quickly." And organizations have had to learn to innovate like crazy; if they don't, they quickly find themselves losing opportunities in the markets in which they operate, as new competition moves in.

Innovation resulting from the ability to move quickly has become an ability mastered by many leading organizations. Consider Rubbermaid. This company introduces 365 new products every year; that's more than one new product every working day. Sony invents 1,000 new products every year, and GE files more patents than any other American organization. And the most dramatic example is perhaps Hewlett Packard. It innovates so much that one-third of its revenues come from lines of business that did not even exist two years ago!

> **Information transformed into knowledge will be the key to success in the 1990s. Raw data floating around will not help businesses make the fast short-term decisions they will need to compete, nor will undigested facts tucked into a computer's memory aid in the long-range planning that will be necessary to move profitably into the next century.**
>
> Ronald D. Rotstein, *The Future — Trends and Developments Through the 21st Century* (a Lyle Stuart book, published by Carol Publishing Group, New Jersey, 1990)

To achieve such constant innovation, a necessity in today's fast world of business, companies have to learn how to constantly re-invent what it is they do. Often, this can only come from ensuring that they have developed an environment that supports innovation, which itself comes from building a culture and method by which people through the company can share and access each other's knowledge.

The knowledge organization, a new, lightning-fast company, constantly innovating, survives and thrives on its ability to harness and harvest the knowledge of its employees. It is a model that all organizations are finding themselves having to subscribe to as we enter the era of the knowledgeable corporation.

Back in 1988, in the accounting firm for which I worked, I started up a project that I called "Linkage." The intent was to unite professionals in various disciplines throughout the company through an electronic mail network, so that they could share their own specialized knowledge. Many others had already begun their own informal networks; computer specialists across the country, for example, had been trading tips and ideas online for years. We found that tax professionals across the country were already plugging into each other, electronically exchanging their thoughts and reactions to the latest federal budget or new tax regulation.

My belief was that the "linkage" concept would provide the impetus for massive information sharing throughout the company, with the result that the business could better respond to clients, deal with competitive pressures and survive in an increasingly complicated world. I still passionately believe in the "linkage" concept today and see many thousands of organizations worldwide implement such projects.

But even back then the concept of "linkage" was not well understood by many in management. I was involved in many international projects and could see the benefit of global information sharing. But when my boss and I flew to New York to make a pitch to senior management, asking them to sponsor the project, which would encourage such information sharing on a global scale, our pitch was met with blank stares. They simply could not comprehend the concept that would capture the imagination of much of the rest of the corporate world through the next decade, even though they understood the competition was already moving rapidly to put in place such technologies.

Returning home from New York, dejected and flabbergasted, the trip turned out to be a first step in my decision years later to walk away from my 12-year career with the company. I simply could not live with what I believed to be blind stupidity.

Today, of course, corporate knowledge — the combined experience, wisdom and awareness held by employees — has come to be recognized as an increasingly important resource and asset. Every leading-edge company, including, finally, my previous employer, has put in place sophisticated knowledge-sharing tools. As they are doing so, they are seeing even greater upheaval in the corporate workplace.

> **We are rapidly shifting from a work force that produces products to one that primarily manages information.... As companies continue to downsize, they will be less willing to pay for "managerial purists"—people who do nothing but manage. Instead, managers will be expected to contribute technical expertise to their jobs and to be willing to roll up their sleeves and contribute when necessary.**
>
> "The new millennium workplace: Seven changes that will challenge managers—and workers," *The Futurist,* March/April, 1996

Before the computer revolution, many companies did not seem to place a high value on the knowledge generated by their staff. Few companies had put in place the sophisticated document tracking and retrieval systems that would let people throughout the company find and locate useful information. Documents, reports, research papers and other valuable information were to be found in filing cabinets or on employees' desks, if they could be found at all. Finding and accessing the talent of people throughout the company was a hit-and-miss solution at best. In effect, one of the most important corporate assets — the collective knowledge and wisdom of employees of the company — was often out of reach and unattainable.

And in those days, many employees justified their existence through their ability to access and harness that knowledge. The result was often that companies lost valuable information on a daily basis, a loss that over time was truly immense. After all, many companies are in the business of using information daily; they generate it over and over. But back then, companies often did not store it, distribute it or re-use it. The drain on their resources as a result of their failure to capture and store corporate knowledge must have been immense.

Then companies began to implement sophisticated computer technology, often involving things such as electronic mail, databases and something known as "groupware," which would permit employees to share information throughout the organization and to keep electronic copies of that information.

Companies soon found that such technologies led to significant changes in the way the organization worked. For many, it was nothing less than a huge cultural shock. Instead of finding that information flowed up and down the hierarchy, from a staff member to a middle manager somewhere over to another middle manager and back down to a staff member, companies discovered that information began to flow freely, throughout the organization, without restraint.

In essence, they discovered that the new computer technologies permitted the rapid and diverse exchange of knowledge and information throughout the organization and more importantly, perhaps, helped the company to capture that all important and elusive resource.

Leading-edge companies began to do what they could to capture such corporate knowledge and build it into electronic databases so that it could be accessed by anyone. And they soon realized that if they could use technology to share the corporate knowledge, the potential of the company would be immeasurably enhanced. In effect, the era of the knowledgeable corporation had begun, as the business world discovered that they could bring together the minds of the people throughout the organization.

The trend towards downsizing is set to continue, as companies continue to discover the power of being a knowledgeable organization. Predictions are that downsizing will continue unabated, much of it due to this new-found capability for sharing information on a widespread basis throughout the company.

> A typical large business in 2010 will have fewer than half the management levels of its counterpart today and about one-third the number of managers.
> • Middle management will all but disappear as information flows directly up to higher management for analysis.
> • Downsizing, restructuring, reorganizations, and cutbacks of white-collar workers will continue until the late 1990s.
> • Computers and information-management systems have stretched the manager's effective span of control from six to 21 employees; thus, fewer mid-level managers are needed.
>
> "An American renaissance in the year 2000: 74 trends that will affect America's future — And Yours," *The Futurist,* March/April, 1994

In essence, through the last 20 years, the business world has discovered that computer technology, which permits the rapid dissemination of knowledge and information throughout the company, can cut through organizational hierarchies that were tens or hundreds of years old.

And there is no doubt that your opportunity for survival in the information age will come from the ability to work in organizations that begin to exploit the power of information technology to provide for corporate-wide knowledge access.

> **As more rank-and-file operations are "informated," employers are increasingly required to pay the 15% to 20% labor market wage premium typically commanded by computer-competent workers.**
> "The revolution in the workplace: What's happening to our jobs?"
> *The Futurist*, March/April, 1996

It will come from your ability to function within a knowledge-based organization and your willingness to accept the change that it brings to the way in which the company works.

What must you do?

1. Grasp and master the new information-sharing tools that are emerging in companies, rather than fighting them.

2. Comprehend, and accept, the cultural change that is occurring in business as the result of the use of such tools. It's important to recognize that a new form of business culture has emerged based on electronic project teams, rather than traditional hierarchies and departments.

3. Learn how to be a participant in knowledge sharing; don't sit on the sidelines! Recognize that a lot of corporate projects now occur electronically through such computer tools and be willing to take part.

22

Rising Above the Crowd

*For Dustin Hoffman, as The Graduate in 1967,
the future was plastics. Today you might say it's plasticity:
the ability to adjust and learn.*

Thomas A. Stewart, "Welcome to the revolution,"
FORTUNE, December 13, 1993

Here's a simple quiz: when corporate downsizing begins, who do you suppose is first on the chopping block: the employee who resists the emergence of the information age or the one who accepts and embraces it? The answer should be obvious.

Our work world is set to change, and to be a survivor, you've got to be willing to change with it. There are many things that you can do to motivate yourself, to take charge of your own personal working life and skills and develop an attitude that will help you to be a survivor. Let's look at some of them.

Changing your attitude towards the information age is probably the most important step that you can undertake. If you have a mental barrier to the possibilities of the era, you likely won't be in a frame of mind to discover success.

Adopt a Positive Attitude About the Information Age

So many of our problems in living through this new age of the wired world have to do with our attitude: we've conditioned ourselves to be negative about anything having to do with the information age. As we have seen, a lot of this is due to the unique upbringing that we have had with the computer revolution.

It is all too easy to be negative about what is happening around us. After all, what is positive about ongoing layoffs, job restructuring and corporate reorganizations? And given our experiences with computer technology to date, with lousy manuals, confusing software and an industry that often shames us into feeling that we are stupid, it's simple to think that it is all a waste of time and that we needn't bother with it.

> **Attitude: It is not the position, but the disposition.**
>
> Unknown

You will not be a survivor if you adopt such an attitude. To prepare for change, you have to be willing to accept change, and the first step in doing that is to have a positive outlook about life and about the opportunities of the information age. Focus your mental energies on identifying the opportunities that are open to you, rather than concentrating on how you might be adversely affected. Seek the upside, not the downside.

Accept the Inevitability of Technological Change

To survive the information age, you must accept that technology will continue to dramatically change our lives. Don't close your mind to the change that will occur; embrace it!

> **Adopting the right attitude can convert a negative stress into a positive one.**
>
> Dr. Hans Selye

Too many people resist the change that is occurring all around us, and as we have seen, they are all too often the first casualties. I have no doubt that the next decade will be pivotal in the history of the way the business community applies computer technology and that the economy in which we work will become increasingly wired together. The impact that we have seen, whether it be electronic commerce, knowledge sharing, new forms of business organization or something else, upon our jobs today will be even greater tomorrow.

Recognize and accept this fact, and you will have come a long way to being a survivor in the information age. A willingness to accept the future, rather than denying it, is the next step to becoming a survivor in the information age.

Seek Success Stories and Learn From Them
Seek out the information age winners, and listen to their stories of success. With some 20 or 30 years of the information age behind us, there are many people who have managed to turn some type of negative career change into a stunning turnaround of dramatic success.

Find the people who have managed to deploy information technology effectively and built their small businesses. Look at home-based business entrepreneurs, who have learned to leverage the power of information technology as a key linchpin of their success. Find those who have developed and mastered the skills of topic tracking and knowledge research and think about what they have accomplished.

Seek out such people and listen to their stories. They have a lot to offer in terms of their own experience. You can learn a lot of valuable information age survival skills by listening to the stories of their own struggles and decisions and by emulating what they have done.

Get Moving, Get Motivated
Don't limit yourself to technology people; motivational speakers, books and tapes are a good source of inspiration in the way that we should think. Although quite often they tell a message that is simple common sense, they encourage us to change our ways, by help-

ing us to focus on the positive things in life, rather than the negative ones.

Peter Legge, in his book *You Can If You Believe You Can* (Eaglet Publishing, Burnaby, B.C., 1995), noted that "I believe that as well as trying, I must strive. I won't go along with the naysayers, with those who don't give a rip. I will dig down deep, to strive, to push myself. And because of all this, I will support my promise to myself to be the best I can be." That's what motivation is all about.

If you've struggled along with technology, but still feel that there is a lot that you can be doing to master the information age, then you need a tug, something to pull yourself along. You need some motivation and some encouragement. Motivation is a funny thing, since it is something that can only come from within. Only you can decide to motivate yourself to discover the magic that lies in the information age for you.

Listen to Visionaries

It's been all too easy to poke fun at those who have made predictions in the past that haven't quite come true. But we can learn from erroneous past predictions, since going back in history helps us to understand our unique attitude to information technology.

As we have seen, trying to predict the future impact of information technology is as difficult as predicting the weather beyond a few days. We know that we'll have more of it, but we are not quite sure exactly what it will be. What can we learn from those who purport to tell us the future? We know from experience that they will not be precise and will often be incorrect. But by listening to what they say, we can form our own judgements and opinions of how the future might evolve. More importantly,

> **First and foremost, your ability to achieve success at a targeted, predetermined goal will be a direct function of the degree of consistent intensity which drives the momentum of your efforts.**
>
> Pete Johnson

by listening to their messages, we are opening our minds up to the future, rather than closing them in the past. A famous saying goes, "People are changed, not by coercion or intimidation, but by example." That's why listening to visionaries can be useful.

Adopt Tenacity as a Weapon
Don't give up! It's easy to suffer a setback in the information age and to use that as an excuse to slow down your momentum. When I walked out of that computer store after failing to buy some computer memory, I felt dejected and embarrassed. Until I reminded myself that I was dealing with a person with an attitude and decided that this one person would not change my determination to master a small task in the information age.

No matter what type of job or career you may have, odds are that it is going to change dramatically through the next several years. The best way to cope with job change is to accept it, anticipate it and work to accommodate it.

Accept Constant Change and Uncertainty in Your Career
You must immediately throw away your concept of a secure career and recognize that in all likelihood, you will face continual, constant change throughout the rest of your working life. What you will be doing tomorrow will likely be very different from what you do today. There's a good chance that you won't even know what is expected of you.

Adopt an attitude that at some point, you will likely have to find a new job, or even a new career, and begin preparing for that eventuality with a positive outlook! Prepare for that eventuality now. What will happen when you find yourself on the street? Will you be ready? Will you have the important information technology skills that will help you to bounce back? Will you be in the right frame of mind to take advantage of the opportunities in front of you, rather than

> ...while it can be hard to watch and be part of change, there's really nothing we can do to stop it. The acceptance of life's passages and the challenges they offer is really a big part of what living life is all about.
>
> Peter Legge, How to Soar with the Eagles (Eaglet Publishing, Burnaby, B.C., 1992)

dwelling on your anger and frustration with the situation in which you find yourself?

You must be willing to change quickly. Given the rapid rate of change in the business world, it will be imperative that your skills, capabilities and attitudes evolve at the same rate that the company that you work for changes.

Anticipate the Future of Your Job

One way to deal with the stress of a technology-induced career or job change is to anticipate it. Monitor the future in order to determine how it might impact you! Take a look around the company in which you work, and think about the changes that are already occurring. How might such developments impact you? Is there a strong likelihood that there are trends underway that are soon to result in a significant change to the way your job is performed or will forever change the fundamentals of your job? If so, what can you do now to plan for that eventuality, in order to be a survivor, instead of a casualty?

This might take some study. Take a broad look at the future, by examining the changes occurring in the industry or profession in which you work. Examine publications or attend conferences in which people report on how your industry is changing and figure out how that change might impact you directly. Undertake such research on the Internet or visit your local library. However you do it, get it done. Do your own crystal-ball gazing and learn from it!

Adapt to Teamwork

Accept and embrace the change already occurring in the workforce today. The trend towards knowledge and information sharing in the corporate world is a dramatic one and is leading to significant cultural change throughout the workplace. The corporate structures that are several hundred years old are not being smashed for the fun of it; they are being destroyed because the new, networked and knowledgeable organization is one that is necessary in today's complex business world. The business organization of yesterday is gone, kaput, dead, and major new types of organizations are emerging in their ashes.

Participate; don't fight such efforts! What is emerging in the corporate workforce is a new form of teamwork, in which groups of people are brought together on a temporary basis through electronic means to tackle some project or issue. The ability to master the technology that supports such interaction is an important skill, but even more important is being a team player! Accept the cultural change that accompanies such efforts; learn to be a participant rather than a viewer on the sidelines!

Throw Out Your Old Work Habits

View a negative job change as positive. For every information technology project, seek out the benefits, rather than concentrating on how it might go wrong. Make suggestions, give advice and don't be afraid to play a role. Our upbringing has conditioned us to be negative about computer technology, and we can see that in the way we deal with the emerging work world. Toss out that baggage and start anew!

Adopt a Realistic Measure of Success

For a long time, many of us have measured our career success by symbols: a corner office with a view, two secretaries and a golf or health club membership. I have my own measure of success: I get to watch two squirrels battle it out in the yard every day and can watch my children wrestle at lunch. Like many people who work in a home office and who have carved out new careers, we judge our success by matters that are far less material than the symbols of yesterday.

You must be willing to throw away the old accoutrements of the past and recognize that success today is more about survival — and lifestyle — than it is about the old status symbols of yesterday.

You must be able to master information technology in order to be a survivor in the age of information.

I have had one formal computer course in my life, and since it was back in 1977, it was rather useless at that. Everything that I do is self-taught. My wife constantly complains that I don't refer to manuals, and that is true. When I get a new program, I simply plunge right in, trying to figure out what it does.

I'm not a genius. I'm not a computer specialist. I've simply adopted the perspective that I want to figure these things out and determine how they can work best in the achievement of my objectives. You can do the same thing and massively upgrade your information technology skills as a result.

> **Having once decided to achieve a certain task, achieve it at all costs of tedium and distaste. The gain in self-confidence of having accomplished a tiresome labour is immense.**
>
> Dr. Thomas Arnold Bennett

Adopt a Willingness to Learn and Upgrade

One of the ways that you can accomplish this is by having a simple and basic willingness — even a desire — to learn. The information age is such that you will find it necessary to continuously upgrade your skills and capabilities. You must adopt an attitude that you will continuously learn new things, and then you must always learn what it is you should be learning!

If you monitor the future correctly, you should have a good understanding of what types of skills you might need in the future. Once you anticipate them, develop them! If you see something new coming, figure out what technology skills might be necessary to let you participate or survive.

You should concentrate on developing "portable" skills. If there is a strong likelihood that you will move from job to job and from career to career, then it would make sense to develop skills that can travel with you.

> **Upgrade your skills. You can't ever afford to rest on the skills you learned in high school or college.**
>
> Peter Legge, You Can If You Believe You Can (Eaglet Publishing, Burnaby, B.C., 1995)

The computer revolution is a constant game of catch-up, and you must continually reinvent what you can do. Accepting this, by adopting the perspective that life will now be a continuous learning process, is a good way to stay ahead of the game.

Develop "Just-in-time" Knowledge Capabilities

Harness the by-products of the information age, immense volumes of information, and put them to use. The information age means that we have a flood of information, some of which will be directly relevant or beneficial to your own survival. Learn how to master the tools of the information age to find and access information when necessary; turn it into knowledge.

Research skills, something that you might not have had to draw upon since you did that last university term paper or high school science project, are becoming a key skill in the information age. I'd recommend you brush up on them!

Above all, refuse to be like the naysayers around you when it comes to the information age, and don't succumb to peer pressure. You should seek to rise above the crowd of techno-doomsters and embrace the new era; it's the best way to avoid the dead ends encountered by all the techno-peasants of our time.

What is important beyond all of these things is that you set goals to ensure that you spend every working day adapting to survival in the information age. You must establish a plan that will help you get personally involved. When you do this, make sure that:

1. You set goals that are specific for the short and long term. You have to set the short-term goals in order to be able to meet the long-term goals. Break down your goals into smaller steps that can be reached in the next week or the next month. If your goals are too big or too far in the future, they might seem unreachable.

> **Goals need to be realistic so you can accept them subconsciously.**
>
> Peter Legge, How to Soar with the Eagles (Eaglet Publishing, Burnaby, B.C., 1992)

2. You set goals that are attainable and realistic. Don't reach too far, too fast!

3. You congratulate yourself on each goal that you achieved. Set a reward for yourself. And if you achieve that goal, take the reward, whether it be a night out or the purchase of a new piece of software. Incentives are always good to have!

4. You make the commitment to yourself that you are going to achieve your goals. The only person you are going to let down by not doing what you set out to do is yourself. If you don't take care of yourself, no one else will.

If occasionally you need some encouragement, look at the children of today. Adopt their attitude in your approach to technology. They do all the right things; they seek out the positive experiences, not the negative ones. And they set out to figure it out; little setbacks don't hold them back. They have a sense of wonder and excitement when exposed to something new, and they don't suffer from a lot of the preconceived notions that we might suffer from when it comes to computer technology. Putting back some of that childhood enthusiasm into our lives may be what we need to survive in the information age.

23

Achieving Hope

I have heard it said that the first ingredient of success — the earliest spark in the dreaming youth — is this; dream a great dream.

John Alan Appleman

There are millions of success stories in the information age. Many of them belong to people like you, folks who have managed to make their way through all the trials and tribulations of the computer age and who have mastered the skills and capabilities that are necessary to survive and succeed in this new era. Why are they successful? What is their secret?

I believe that it is their enthusiasm for the new era and the determination with which they throw themselves at mastering the information age instead of being slaves to it. They've discovered their own magic, and they can be a beacon of hope for the rest of us.

We have all hit low points, been in situations in which events in our lives and our careers have overtaken us to a point that we lose that

Achieving Hope

> **When you determine what you want, you have made the most important decision of your life. You have to know what you want in order to attain it.**
>
> Douglas Lurtan

most important of all human characteristics, hope. To survive in the information age, you must have hope; it's the most basic of human necessities. Give yourself hope, and you can have everything — confidence, ability, skill, enthusiasm, determination. Hope is the fuel that drives us to the future. But hope is a funny thing; you often have to work hard to find it.

I remember when I hit my low point, dramatically and with full force, shortly after the company merger in 1989. This event, at the time, seemed to effectively destroy everything that I had been working towards for five years.

Life was certain; I knew exactly what was coming and where I was going. Until, of course, events beyond my control ripped those plans away from me. Suddenly, the future, which I thought I had all mapped out, didn't exist anymore. I didn't know what was coming, and I didn't know what I would do.

As the negative impact of the change in my job took hold, a sense of gloom descended upon me. I knew I no longer wanted to stay with that firm, but I didn't have a clue what I would do next. Within weeks I had decided to quit, but couldn't bring myself to do it. And through the next nine months, I actually decided two or three times to quit and then always backed off at the last minute, because I was terrified of the future.

When you don't know what the future will bring you, you lose hope. That's what happened to me. I lost my confidence, the worst possible thing that could happen at the time. I lost sight of my abilities. I no longer had a good idea of what I could do. I was unsure of my skills and didn't know what type of company might be interested in hiring me.

Uncertainty built upon uncertainty. Many painful days and sleepless nights were spent trying to figure out what I should do with my career. Should I quit? Should I look for another job? Should I start my own consulting business? What should I do?

Losing confidence in yourself — because you've lost hope — is a terrible thing! Particularly when you are trying to carve out a new career, when you are trying to be a survivor. "I don't know what my skills are," I would cry out to my wife in moments of frustration. "I don't know what it is I can do! Who would want to hire me?" I pleaded. And in anger and frustration, I damned the forces that caused such an upheaval in my career. My loss of hope was such that over time, I convinced myself that I had little to offer the corporate world and that I was staring at a dead-end future. What a miserable state of mind to be in!

Be the best you can be. Get the most from every day. Success has nothing to do with I.Q. It's just doing a little more every day. It's aptitude and attitude.

Peter Legge, How to Soar with the Eagles (Eaglet Publishing, Burnaby, B.C., 1992)

But I did finally leave my job, and it didn't take me that long to come to the conclusion that walking away from that job and establishing my own business was the best thing that I had ever done!

I remember the day when the enormity of what I had accomplished hit home. It was about a year after I had quit. It was 6:45 a.m. on a spring day. The sun was coming up, the birds were singing, a warm breeze was blowing in the window, a steaming cup of coffee on the desk. I had just gone through my voice mail and had heard very positive news from three potential clients. Although my business was still very new and the risk was high, the signs were that I would succeed.

Your hope can be found in the fact that so many others have taken advantage of the technology of the information age to accomplish their own magic.

For years, I've had the wonderful opportunity of traveling the country and speaking to tens of thousands of Canadians, describing to them my sense of wonder at the opportunities for personal success in the information age. And inevitably, every time I speak to a crowd, someone comes up to me afterwards to tell me about something that he or she has managed to accomplish in the information age. Building his own Internet Web site. Learning how to do online research. Computerizing her business. Establishing a home office, and managing it with a computer. Doing the family tree on the computer.

I listen carefully, always eager to hear another wonderful success story. Consequently, I have met thousands who have managed to turn this challenging and changing world into a fantastic personal opportunity, not a ball and chain around the neck of their careers.

> **We promise according to our hopes and perform according to our fears.**
> Author unknown

What has struck me most about all of these people is their enthusiasm; they are convinced they have found something wonderful. And they have. They have discovered that there is hope in this new era through the mastery of the technology of the information age.

After all, they can undertake electronic research and are slowly teaching themselves to obtain "just-in-time" knowledge. They have learned how to effectively use technologies like the Internet to enhance their skills and capabilities. They are learning to effectively apply information technology to their businesses, in order to achieve some efficiencies in the day-to-day operations of the company, to save money or to achieve some type of lasting competitive advantage. They have learned to use it for personal fun, translating their hobby into a worldwide project.

At some point, they managed to get beyond their fears and intimidation and have thrown away the baggage of the past. They have plodded their way through the lousy manuals, confusing software and hubris of the computer revolution and have triumphed over the technology.

> We grow great by dreams. All big men are dreamers. They see things in the soft haze of a spring day or in the red fire of a long winter's evening. Some of us let these great dreams die, but others nourish and protect them; nurse them through bad days till they bring them to the sunshine and light which comes always to those who sincerely hope that their dreams will come true.
> Woodrow Wilson

And in doing so, they have become survivors — not casualties — of the information age. Whatever they have managed to do, I see a common key characteristic in these people: they have discovered the true magic of the information age, that it truly is something that leads to personal and business enrichment.

They have come to fulfill the potential found in the adage "what lies behind us and what lies before us are tiny matters compared to what lies within us."

The future isn't bleak; in fact, it is truly wonderful, but only if you decide to make it so. What you need to do to be a survivor in the information age, beyond everything else — your attitude, skills and capabilities — is to give yourself some hope.

The hope that you can master the technology of the information age, that you can survive the new forms of corporate organization that are emerging and the hope that you can enhance and develop your career, job and personal skills.

By doing what is necessary to survive in the information age, you can prosper

> **Hope is both the earliest and the most indispensable virtue inherent in the state of being alive. If life is to be sustained hope must remain, even where confidence is wounded, trust impaired.**
>
> Erik H. Erikson

from the riches that it offers. The information age is out there, all around you, encompassing everything you do. The true secret is that it is up to you to go and find it

How can I close this book and offer you the hope that you need to find your own success and survival in the information age? By offering these simple words of encouragement: you can do it! You can master the technology and develop the skills necessary to survive this new era. May some hope be with you.

Coming Soon!

Thriving in the Information Age

by Jim Carroll, CA

A sequel to *Surviving the Information Age*, *Thriving in the Information Age* is scheduled for release in Spring 1998.

In this informative new book, Jim expands on the enormous opportunities available for personal achievement as the information age takes hold. With a clear focus on the world of work, Jim details how new technology is drastically changing the rules that guided us in the past. He shows how business is being permanently changed by the direct interaction between consumers and suppliers. He also explores how new organizations are literally forming overnight—presenting traditional business with a whole new set of competitors!

Jim uses his specialized experience in business and technology to provide the reader with a glimpse into the future, identifying some of the technologies, trends and careers that will emerge in the next 25 years. In doing so, he helps us to understand how we can position ourselves for enormous personal and professional growth.

Lively, engaging and concise, *Thriving in the Information Age* demonstrates how the emerging wired economy is forever changing the North American business landscape. It will be of tangible benefit to those with the insight to think strategically about their place in this exciting new world.

Watch for *Thriving in the Information Age*—coming soon to a bookstore near you!

Surviving the Information Age!
With Presentations by Jim Carroll!

If you like this book, you'll love a presentation by Jim Carroll!

The book's key inspirational message—and Jim's characteristic stories, suggestions and guidance—will add an exciting and powerful dimension to your next conference, seminar or corporate meeting. Help everyone in your organization cope with the emerging information age, with a presentation by Jim Carroll.

Jim Carroll is recognized as one of North America's leading speakers. The author of over 14 books, he has earned a significant reputation as a highly charged and exciting speaker—audiences rave about his enthusiastic performances!

In the past several years, Jim Carroll has been retained for keynote presentations and seminars by many influential and high-profile organizations, a sample of which includes:

Alberta Association for Continuing Education • Alberta Department of Economic Development and Tourism • Alberta Library Association • American Marketing Association • Bay Networks • Business Development Bank of Canada • Canadian Association of Broadcasters • Canadian Association of Credit Unions • Canadian Association of Mortgage Financing • Canadian Association of Petroleum Landmen • Canadian Bar Association • Canadian Broadcast Executives Association • Canadian Community Newspaper Association • Canadian Corporate News • Canadian Finance and Leasing Association • Canadian Home Builders Association • Canadian Imperial Bank of Commerce • Canadian Information Processing Society • Canadian Institute of Chartered Accountants • Canadian Investor Relations Institute • Canadian Library Association • Canadian Society of Association Executives • Canadian Society of Magazine Editors • Canadian Treasury Management Association • Confectionery Manufacturers Association of Canada • Credit Union Central Alberta • Credit Union Central Manitoba • Credit Union Directors of Ontario • Credit Union Management Association of Ontario • Digital Equipment • Durham Regional Manufacturers Association • Grant McEwan Community College • Great West Life • Health Administration Association of BC • Hewlett Packard •

Continued

Human Resources Professional Association of Ontario • IBM • Investment Funds Institute of Canada • IREV (Swedish Accounting Association) • Metro Halifax Chamber of Commerce • Montreal Trust • Northern Telecom • Northwestern Ontario Economic Development Network • Ontario Hospital Association • Ontario Municipal Social Services Association • Ontario Science Centre • Patent and Trademark Institute of Canada • Planning Forum • Professional Marketing Research Society • Propane Gas Association of Canada • Purchasing Management Association of Canada • Queens University Executive Program • Royal Bank of Canada • Saskatchewan Economic Development • Saskatchewan Indian Federated College • Saskatchewan Power • Scotia MacLeod • Toronto Board of Trade • Treasury Management Association of Canada • Western Retail Lumbermen's Association • Winnipeg Chamber of Commerce • Winnipeg Free Press • World Congress of Association Executives • Yorkton Securities • Young Presidents Organization – Atlantic Chapter

Jim Carroll is represented by the National Speakers Bureau, an organization which represents some of Canada's most high profile and dynamic speakers.

National Speakers Bureau

Phone 1-800-661-4110/604-224-2384
Fax 604-224-8906
Web site **www.nsb.com**
E-mail **speakers@nsb.com**

Jim Carroll

Phone 905-855-2950
Fax 905-855-0269
Web site **www.jimcarroll.com**
E-mail **jcarroll@jimcarroll.com**

Be sure to check out the
Surviving the Information Age Web site, at
www.jimcarroll.com

Credits

Chapter 1
"Computers: Is There a God?" From *Newsweek*, January 10, 1966, Newsweek Inc. All rights reserved. Reprinted by permission, page 67.

Chapter 2
"Microcomputers and Young Children: An Interactive View," by Greta G. Fein. *Young Children and Microcomputers,* edited by Patricia F. Campbell and Greta G. Fein. Copyright 1986. All rights reserved. Allyn and Bacon.

"The 'Computer Revolution' in Education: A Research Perspective," by Mark R. Lepper and James D. Milojkovic. *Young Children and Microcomputers,* edited by Patricia F. Campbell and Greta G. Fein. Copyright 1986. All rights reserved. Allyn and Bacon.

Chapter 3
"The revolution in the workplace: What's happening to our jobs?" Originally appeared in the March/April 1996 issue of *The Futurist*. Used with permission from the World Future Society, 7910 Woodmount Avenue, Suite 450, Bethesda, Maryland, pages 8-13.

Harmony: Business, Technology & Life After Paperwork, Arno Penzias, Harper Business, A Division of HarperCollins Publishers Inc. Copyright © 1995 by Arno Penzias, pages 6-7.

Chapter 4
From *The 7 Habits of Highly Effective People* by Stephen R. Covey. Copyright © 1989 by Stephen R. Covey. A Fireside Book published by Simon & Schuster, page 75.

Chapter 6
Extract taken from *The Dream Machine: Exploring the Computer Age* by Jon Palfreman & Doron Swade, with the permission of BBC Worldwide Limited. Copyright © 1991, page 127.

From *The Future: Trends and Developments Through the 21st Century* by Ronald D. Rotstein. Copyright © 1990 by Ronald D. Rotstein. A Lyle Stuart Book published by arrangement by Carol Publishing Group, pages 33-34.

Chapter 7
"The Big Whir: Computers Spin Problems and Profits." From *Newsweek*, October 21, 1963, Newsweek Inc. All rights reserved. Reprinted by permission, page 92.

Extract taken from *The Dream Machine: Exploring the Computer Age* by Jon Palfreman & Doron Swade, with the permission of BBC Worldwide Limited. Copyright © 1991, page 44.

Extract taken from *The Dream Machine: Exploring the Computer Age* by Jon Palfreman & Doron Swade, with the permission of BBC Worldwide Limited. Copyright © 1991, pages 68-69.

"It's Here—The Computer Revolution." Condensed from *National Geographic* by Peter T. White, *Readers Digest*, May 1971.

Chapter 8
Boston Computer Society, THINGS THE MANUAL NEVER TOLD YOU, pages xi & 3. © 1985 The Boston Computer Society. Reprinted by permission of Addison-Wesley Longman Inc.

Harmony: Business, Technology & Life After Paperwork, Arno Penzias, Harper Business, A Division of HarperCollins Publishers Inc., Copyright © 1995 by Arno Penzias, Introduction, page xiii.

Harmony: Business, Technology & Life After Paperwork, Arno Penzias, Harper Business, A Division of HarperCollins Publishers Inc., Copyright © 1995 by Arno Penzias, page 97.

Chapter 9

The Design of Everyday Things, Donald A. Norman. Basic Books, A Division of HarperCollins Publishing Inc. Copyright © 1988 by Donald A. Norman, Preface, page xi.

The Design of Everyday Things, Donald A. Norman. Basic Books, A Division of HarperCollins Publishing Inc. Copyright © 1988 by Donald A. Norman, Preface, pages 179-180.

Extract taken from *The Dream Machine: Exploring the Computer Age* by Jon Palfreman & Doron Swade, with the permission of BBC Worldwide Limited. Copyright © 1991, pages 95-96.

Chapter 10

Albert Mehrabian, Ph.D., Professor of Psychology. From Professor Albert Mehrabian's Web page, http://www.wp.com/mehrab. Reproduced by permission.

Chapter 11

"Consider the PC Paradox." From *Newsweek*, February 27. © 1995, Newsweek Inc. All rights reserved. Reprinted by permission, page 48.

Editor's Comments, Blake Ives. Reprinted by special permission from the *MIS Quarterly*, Volume 18, Number 2, June 1994. Copyright 1994 by the Society of Information Management and the Management Information Systems Research Center at the University of Minnesota.

Chapter 12

Boston Computer Society, THINGS THE MANUAL NEVER TOLD YOU, pages xi & 3. © 1985 The Boston Computer Society. Reprinted by permission of Addison-Wesley Longman Inc.

Chapter 13

Extract taken from *The Dream Machine: Exploring the Computer Age* by Jon Palfreman & Doron Swade, with the permission of BBC Worldwide Limited. Copyright © 1991, page 32.

From *The Devouring Fungus: Tales of the Computer Age* by Karla Jennings. Copyright © 1990 by Karla Jennings. Reprinted by permission of W.W. Norton & Company, Inc., page 123.

"Hacker Ethics," Neal Patrick, in *Digital Deli* edited by Steve Ditlea. Workman Publishing Company Inc. Copyright © 1984, page 62.

From *The Devouring Fungus: Tales of the Computer Age* by Karla Jennings. Copyright © 1990 by Karla Jennings. Reprinted by permission of W.W. Norton & Company, Inc., page 68.

Chapter 14

"A Brief History of Artificial Intelligence," Stephanie Haack, in *Digital Deli* edited by Steve Ditlea. Workman Publishing Company Inc. Copyright © 1984, page 232.

From *Megamistakes: Forecasting and The Myth of Rapid Technological Change* by Steven P. Schnaars. Copyright © 1989 by The Free Press, a Division of Simon & Schuster. Reprinted with permission of the publisher, page 80.

Extract taken from *The Dream Machine: Exploring the Computer Age* by Jon Palfreman & Doron Swade, with the permission of BBC Worldwide Limited. Copyright © 1991, pages 78-79.

"Machines Are This Smart." From *Newsweek*, October 24. © 1960, Newsweek Inc. All rights reserved. Reprinted by permission, pages 85-87.

Extract taken from *The Dream Machine: Exploring the Computer Age* by Jon Palfreman & Doron Swade, with the permission of BBC Worldwide Limited. Copyright © 1991, pages 168-169.

"Why Work?" From *Newsweek*, February 12. © 1962, Newsweek Inc. All rights reserved. Reprinted by permission.

"Human Race Predicted to Die in Favor of 'Living' Robots/Marry a Robot? Futurist Says Yes by Year 2000." Copyright 1982 and 1985 by Computerworld, Inc. Framingham, MA 01701. Reprinted from Computerworld.

From *Megamistakes: Forecasting and The Myth of Rapid Technological Change* by Steven P. Schnaars. Copyright © 1989 by The Free Press, a Division of Simon & Schuster. Reprinted with permission of the publisher, page 48.

Extract taken from *The Dream Machine: Exploring the Computer Age* by Jon Palfreman & Doron Swade, with the permission of BBC Worldwide Limited. Copyright © 1991, page 56.

From *Megamistakes: Forecasting and The Myth of Rapid Technological Change* by Steven P. Schnaars. Copyright © 1989 by The Free Press, a Division of Simon & Schuster. Reprinted with permission of the publisher, pages 9-10.

Extract taken from *The Dream Machine: Exploring the Computer Age* by Jon Palfreman & Doron Swade, with the permission of BBC Worldwide Limited. Copyright © 1991, page 187.

Chapter 15

"The Great Snafu." From *Newsweek*, September 15. © 1969, Newsweek Inc. All Rights Reserved. Reprinted by permission, page 79.

Extract taken from *The Dream Machine: Exploring the Computer Age* by Jon Palfreman & Doron Swade, with the permission of BBC Worldwide Limited. Copyright © 1991, page 180.

From *The Devouring Fungus: Tales of the Computer Age* by Karla Jennings. Copyright © 1990 by Karla Jennings. Reprinted by permission of W.W. Norton & Company, Inc., pages 190-191.

Ann Landers Column, *Providence RI Journal*, July 1, 1987. Permission granted by Ann Landers/Creators Syndicate.

"Man killed by accident with medical radiation." *Boston Globe*, June 20, 1986. Reprinted courtesy of the *Boston Globe*.

"If a Computer Fouls Up Your Charge Account." Condensed from "Changing Times," *The Kiplinger Magazine, Reader's Digest*, January, 1971.

Chapter 16

"DMV computer error puts innocent motorist in jail." April 1985. Copyright 1982 and 1985 by Computerworld, Inc. Framingham, MA 01701. Reprinted from Computerworld.

Chapter 17

Extract taken from *The Dream Machine: Exploring the Computer Age* by Jon Palfreman & Doron Swade, with the permission of BBC Worldwide Limited. Copyright © 1991, pages 129-130.

"History's Great Computer Eccentrics," Marguerite Zientara. Workman Publishing Company Inc. Copyright © 1984, page 6.

"Why Work?" From *Newsweek*, February 12. © 1962, Newsweek Inc. All rights reserved. Reprinted by permission.

Chapter 18

From *The Future: Trends and Developments Through the 21st Century* by Ronald D. Rotstein. Copyright © 1990 by Ronald D. Rotstein. A Lyle Stuart Book published by arrangement by Carol Publishing Group, pages 3-4.

Chapter 19

Harmony: Business, Technology & Life After Paperwork, Arno Penzias. Harper Business, A Division of HarperCollins Publishers Inc., Copyright © 1995 by Arno Penzias, page 49.

"The revolution in the workplace: What's happening to our jobs?" Originally appeared in the March/April 1996 issue of "The Futurist." Used with permission from the World Future Society, 7910 Woodmount Avenue, Suite 450, Bethesda, Maryland, pages 8-13.

"An American renaissance in the year 2000: 74 trends that will affect America's future—and yours." Originally appeared in the March/April 1994 issue of "The Futurist." Used with permission from the World Future Society, 7910 Woodmount Avenue, Suite 450, Bethesda, Maryland, pages SS1-SS11.

"Welcome to the revolution," Thomas A. Stewart. FORTUNE, © 1993 Time Inc. All rights reserved, pages 66-80.

Chapter 21

"Welcome to the revolution," Thomas A. Stewart. FORTUNE, © 1993 Time Inc. All rights reserved, pages 66-80

The End of Work, Jeremy Rifkin. A Jeremy P. Tarcher/Putman Book published by G. P. Putnam's Sons. Copyright 1995, Introduction, page xvi.

From *The Future: Trends and Developments Through the 21st Century* by Ronald D. Rotstein. Copyright © 1990 by Ronald D. Rotstein. A Lyle Stuart Book published by arrangement by Carol Publishing Group, pages 33-34.

"The new millennium workplace: Seven changes that will challenge managers—and workers." Originally appeared in the March/April 1996 issue of "The Futurist." Used with permission from the World Future Society, 7910 Woodmount Avenue, Suite 450, Bethesda, Maryland, pages 14-18.

"An American renaissance in the year 2000: 74 trends that will affect America's future—and yours." Originally appeared in the March/April 1994 issue of "The Futurist." Used with permission from the World Future Society, 7910 Woodmount Avenue, Suite 450, Bethesda, Maryland, pages SS1-SS11.

"The revolution in the workplace: What's happening to our jobs?" Originally appeared in the March/April 1996 issue of "The Futurist." Used with permission from the World Future Society, 7910 Woodmount Avenue, Suite 450, Bethesda, Maryland, pages 8-13.

Chapter 22

"Welcome to the revolution," Thomas A. Stewart. FORTUNE, © 1993 Time Inc. All rights reserved, pages 66-80.